SUCCESS WITH HYDRANGEAS

Managing Editor: Katie Elzer-Peters

Copy Editor: Billie Brownell

Designer: Nathan Bauer

Proofreader: Billie Brownell

Indexer: Claire Splan

ISBN: 978-0-9820394-2-7

Library of Congress Control Number: 2017916786

Printed in the United States of America

SUCCESS WITH HYDRANGEAS

A GARDENER'S GUIDE

LORRAINE BALLATO

Hydrangea macrophylla 'All Summer Beauty' lives up to its name

DEDICATION

To my husband, Anthony, who has supported me in my horticultural journey throughout the years. You have given me more than courage to pursue this dream.

ACKNOWLEDGMENTS

There are scores of men and women who work on hydrangeas: plant hunters, researchers, breeders, growers, curators, head gardeners at botanical gardens, plant pathologists, nurserymen and -women, and hundreds of others in leadership and supportive roles around the world. All of them collectively have contributed to the body of knowledge we share on hydrangea species and cultivars. Yes, there is a commercial aspect to all of this, but I believe it is the same passion we all share for hydrangeas that drives our collective zeal for working with this plant genus.

Some keep their lights hidden, others shine brightly, and still others are somewhere else along that spectrum, but make no mistake: they all have contributed to the current plant palette, whether it be at the nursery, in display gardens, or somewhere in a laboratory. We owe them a debt of gratitude. If I could thank them all personally I would, but I have only had the good fortune to meet a handful and correspond with maybe another dozen or so—an infinitesimally small number of the total field of contributors.

That small number will have to shoulder the burden of representation for their colleagues. First and foremost is Dr. Michael Dirr, who is always at the ready to confirm or debunk my theories of why our New England plants didn't flower (among other things); Monsieur Robert Mallett of the renowned Shamrock Collection in France; Stacey Hirvela and Tim Wood at Spring Meadow Nursery, who help me understand the finer technical points of hydrangea growth and performance; Dr. Mark T. Windham from the University of Tennessee, who worked with me and helped me better grasp the mysterious world of hydrangea diseases; Ryan McEnaney at Bailey Nurseries, Kevin Cramer at Van Belle Nursery, and Jeanine Standard at Proven Winners Plants®, who make sure I have trial plants. They are all my hydrangea heroes.

I'm sure there are others over the past fifteen years whose brains I have picked and who have generously shared their knowledge and experience about hydrangeas with me. I wish I could recall all of them by name to publicly thank them. But alas, I have had one glass of champagne too many, which has washed away those memories and ask forgiveness for the unintended oversight. And then there are the people who worked so hard to help bring this book into being. Copy editor Billie Brownell, indexer Claire Splan, and designer Nathan Bauer were part of a dream team led by managing editor extraordinaire Katie Elzer-Peters. Her patience and perseverance made it possible for me to get this book into your hands.

One hydrangea can make a stunning statement

TABLE OF CONTENTS

INTRODUCTION

This book is about how to grow hydrangea plants, plain and simple.

It's not about taxonomy, or how to dry them, or how to make a bouquet. It's about how to make your hydrangeas thrive. It's about helping you decide which ones to buy for your garden and, once you get them home, what to do with them—their care and feeding. It's not about distinguishing among the hundreds of options you may find at the garden center or in catalogs. It's about *understanding* the common species you might find at the garden center or elsewhere and be tempted to grow in your garden.

Practical, practical, practical!

Let's start at the beginning. Saddle up!

PLANT NAMES

In this book I refer to hydrangeas by their botanical species names. Why did I write it by species and not the common names of the plants you'll find in the garden centers or catalogs? It's absolutely impossible to keep current on marketplace offerings. You have the internet and mail-order catalogs for that. Each season there will be countless new introductions in your immediate marketplace. Depending upon where in the country you garden and the garden center you go to, in addition to the arrangements that are made between growers and sellers, there's no way of knowing which plants will be offered, or where, at any time. Common names also differ from place to place. Additionally, within species there are dozens of cultivars (cultivated varieties) for which genetic improvements have been made.

With that in mind, I cover the five most common species you're likely to run into and their care. My intent is to give you an idea of what each species is capable of. Always read plant tags and descriptions for specifics about individual plants.

A blue hydrangea and orange daylilies echo a favorite Van Gogh color scheme

The world's leading authority on accurate plant species and subspecies names is a jointly coordinated online publication hosted by the Royal Botanic Gardens, Kew and the Missouri Botanical Garden. Known as The Plant List (www.theplantlist.org), it operates under the auspices of the International Society for Horticultural Science (ISHS); the International Cultivar Registration Authority (ICRA) is appointed for each genus. By registering new cultivars with the ICRA, duplication of cultivar names is avoided, names are kept in accordance with the International Code of Nomenclature for Cultivated Plants, and names are formally established.

What could be more welcoming than these two containers of pink hydrangeas?

It is those names and their associated spellings, taken from The Plant List, that are used in this book:

- *Hydrangea macrophylla*: Hortensia, Mophead, or Lacecap. This section also captures *Hydrangea serrata*: aka Mountain hydrangea

- *Hydrangea quercifolia*: Oakleaf

- *Hydrangea petiolaris*: Climbing

- *Hydrangea arborescens*: Smooth or Woodland

- *Hydrangea paniculata*: Panicle, Pee Gee, (sometimes referred to as *Paniculata grandiflora*)

WHY USE BOTANICAL NAMES?

Botanical names are your keys to the kingdom. Without them, you simply won't know exactly what you are getting or you might not get what you want when shopping. While cultivar names cannot be duplicated, common names can be different from region to region. Botanical names tell you exactly what you need to know. As this relates to hydrangeas, the translation is simple:

- *Macro* = large or big; *phylla* = leaf; therefore, *macrophylla* = big leaf

- *Serrata* = serrated or sawtoothed, as it refers to the leaf

- *Querci* = oak; *folia* = another name for leaf; therefore, *quercifolia* = oakleaf

- *Paniculata* = panicled or having a panicle form of flower (Panicle flowers are loose, open, or branching that bloom from the center or bottom outward or toward the top.)

- *Petiolaris* = with a particularly long leaf stalk (petiole), which in this species allows the plant to develop rootlets for climbing

Now that you understand hydrangea names, we're ready to start!

A lacecap hydrangea gracefully adorns a
wrought iron gate

PART ONE:
GETTING TO KNOW HYDRANGEAS

MEET THE HYDRANGEA TYPES YOU'RE MOST LIKELY TO GROW AND LEARN SOME LINGO TO HELP YOU NAVIGATE THIS BOOK.

Hydrangea macrophyllas do well in seashore environments

CHAPTER ONE

FIVE COMMON HYDRANGEA SPECIES AND THEIR UNIQUE NEEDS

Hydrangea macrophylla
BIG LEAF HYDRANGEA

This is the most popular form of hydrangea, bar none. Native to Japan and Korea, it's the one most often featured in magazines because of its dazzling flowers and sheer loveliness. They do especially well in shoreline communities because of their tolerance for salt air. You can't beat them for the impact they make in a mass planting. Eye candy doesn't even come close to describing it!

You'll find these fabulous blue or pink snowball-like flowers in the landscape in June and in dried bouquets and wreaths anytime. Home decorators frequently use them—and charge a hefty price. You might hear the snowball-like flowers called "mopheads."

These old-fashioned shrubs go by other names, including "hortensia" and "florist's hydrangea." Up until the beginning of this century, plants were only available in the United States that matured to a large size of 5 feet by 5 feet or more. I clearly remember one from my childhood at my grandmother's house that we used to call the "snowball" plant. Try to find that one at the garden center!

Hydrangea macrophylla Endless Summer® 'Blushing Bride'

Hydrangea macrophylla also comes in a lacecap flower form. This flower looks a bit different. At first glance you might think you're looking at an unopened mophead because the flower is made up of an inner circle of fertile (less showy) flowers that look like very tight buds surrounded by an outer ring of sterile flowers. Its flat head has a more delicate look than the traditional mophead, *Hydrangea macrophylla*, flower, but it's no less appealing and functional in a garden setting.

Hydrangea macrophylla lacecap flower

That central area of fertile florets is a bee magnet. Like mopheads, lacecaps used to only be available as large specimens but today's marketplace offers smaller cultivars as well.

You may see a reference to "Teller" when you deal with lacecap varieties. These are plants bred in the 1980s in Switzerland. They originally carried Swiss or German names of birds that translated to "pheasant" or "nightingale." Those old names are rarely used now; more likely you will see "Teller Red" or "Teller Blue." (*Teller* is a German word for "flat.") Many of the original twenty-six species have been lost, leaving us with just a few from which to choose if you even see them at all at garden centers or in catalogs.

Historically, the large size of these plants led owners to think they needed to prune the plants hard and frequently. Unfortunately, this resulted in stems and flowerbuds being removed before they could flower and it prevented plants from generating new buds.

That has changed since the commercial introduction in 2004 of reblooming hydrangeas, which has affected the rules on pruning *Hydrangea macrophylla*. We'll cover this hydrangea pruning question in great detail throughout this chapter so you can rest assured that you will be extremely comfortable pruning all hydrangeas you own as well as any you may get asked about by others.

WHERE TO PLANT *HYDRANGEA MACROPHYLLA*

There is no single answer about where to plant as many factors affect selecting the right location.

Initially, you need to match your growing zone (hardiness zone) to the hardiness zone of the plant you have. Most *Hydrangea macrophylla* plants are hardy to zone 5 and warmer; a few are hardy to zone 4. There is a detailed discussion on hydrangea hardiness in Chapter 11, which should help you better understand hardiness as it relates to hydrangeas.

Then there is sunlight. If you garden in a cold, northern climate like that of zones 4 or 5, plants can take more sun and will, in fact, produce more flowers as long as they get enough moisture and the soil composition is right. I recommend a location that receives six hours of morning sun with some dappled shade in the afternoon.

That doesn't mean that if the only site you have for your *Hydrangea macrophylla* is a border with afternoon sun that it will be a disaster—quite the contrary. You simply have to adapt the plant care to the growing conditions to ensure success. In this case, you will need to closely watch for dehydration and be careful not to overwater to compensate for that scorching afternoon sun. You might even consider planting some fast-growing, protective plants like Kousa dogwoods, beeches, or conifers on the south- or west-facing side of the border, close enough to provide shade to your *Hydrangea macrophylla* within a few years. Make sure, however, that those shade providers are not too close as they will create root competition for precious moisture. I have had great success using *Buddleias* to provide seasonal shade; they grow very quickly in one season but are not water hogs.

The farther south you go, the less a site in direct sun is recommended as the sun will fry your plants and bleach their color. Even in a northern zone 5, all day sun is not recommended due to color bleaching.

In the North, it is preferable to site plants where they'll have some winter protection. *Hydrangea macrophylla* stems and flowerbuds are especially sensitive to icy winter winds, which dry them out. They do better when they are planted on the northern side of structures, or where they can enjoy the protection of persistent winter foliage from plants such as oaks, beeches, or conifers. Again, always be mindful of the root systems of those trees: don't place your hydrangeas so close that they have to compete for essential moisture. Remember, it's shade and winter protection you're after.

HYDRANGEA MACROPHYLLA AND *H. SERRATA* FLOWERS

Many *Hydrangea macrophylla* and *H. serrata* flowers can be manipulated either to be blue or pink, depending on the soil pH, which I'm about to cover. If color isn't important to you, then just aim for a soil pH between 4.5 to 8 to keep your plant happy.

Here's one version of a soil test kit sold at garden centers

Most gardeners, however, have a specific color in mind when they plan their garden and, because of their big showy flowers, hydrangeas can play a role in this color scheme. Therefore, knowing the ins and outs of how pH affects this shrub is basic knowledge. Having your own soil testing kit (easily purchased from most garden centers) is the first step, as is knowing when and how to use it.

You may also want to check the pH of your water, too, especially if you're on a well. Your water source may thwart your best efforts to change the color of your flowers, so get a handle on it before you start.

Now for your science lesson: what is pH? Technically, pH is the logarithmic measure of hydrogen ion concentration. In normal language, it's the scale used to measure the degree of alkalinity and acidity based on a numbering system of 1 through 14, with 7 being neutral. A number below seven is acidic while 8 to 14 is alkaline.

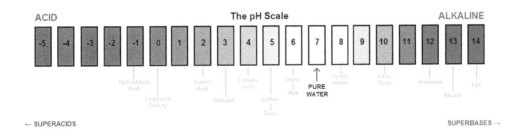

A scale shows the range of pH readings of common items

That pH reading tells you about your plant's ability to absorb aluminum in the soil, which is the real deciding factor for the color of your hydrangea flowers. If the soil is too alkaline, the aluminum gets "tied up" and isn't available to the plant roots, making your *Hydrangea macrophylla* flowers pink. That's why plants at the base of a house foundation or around a concrete walkway are more likely to be pink. The continual leaching from the concrete foundation or walkway affects the soil, making it alkaline. If you have an especially rainy early summer, those flowers you worked so hard to turn blue might fade closer to pink right before your eyes as the adjoining concrete repeatedly gets washed by Mother Nature.

GENERAL INFORMATION ABOUT CHANGING FLOWER COLOR

Don't expect any amendments you add in spring to take effect during the current season. The right time to amend is in fall since the soil needs time to absorb amendments in order to change. Of course, you'll need to continually test and amend on an ongoing basis, possibly each season. Each cultivar responds differently to this soil pH treatment so the "formula" that works for one plant may not be the same for another. Do you really want to take on this annual chore? Maybe you should move the plant to a more hospitable site or learn to love what happens naturally.

Don't necessarily assume that if you buy a pink- or blue-flowered *Hydrangea macrophylla* you can change the color in the future. Many of today's newer cultivars are not pH sensitive. This is generally indicated on the plant tag or description. If causing a hydrangea to flower pink or blue is a choice you want, make sure you purchase a pH-sensitive plant. Some *H. macrophylla* plants are neither pink nor blue, as is the case with the beautiful, pure white 'Madame Emile Mouillère'. No amount of amending will change its flower color, so make sure you know that before you plunk your money down.

Hydrangea macrophylla 'Madame Emile Mouillère'

For Pink Flowers

If you want pink flowers, aim for a soil pH from 6.0 to 6.2. You can use dolomitic lime to reach that pH. If you go too far and the hydrangea leaves start to turn yellow, you might have induced an iron deficiency. Check the soil pH and see where it is. If it's above 6.4, iron deficiency is likely. Consult your local garden center for the right product. Don't worry; it's easily treated and your plant will thank you for it pretty quickly. Fertilizers with high levels of phosphorous might help encourage flowering while preventing the plant from "taking up" aluminum, in turn keeping the flowers pink. However, treating the soil with phosphorous is not one of my favorite methods. It doesn't move easily into the plant and runs off into the environment, polluting waterways and groundwater. I don't recommend it.

Pink *Hydrangea macrophylla* "mystery variety"

For Blue Flowers

On the other hand, a *Hydrangea macrophylla* planted under the protection of pine trees will likely have blue flowers because of the natural soil acidity created by decomposing pine needles. For blue flowers, aim for an acidic pH level of about 5.2 to 5.5. You can even go as low a soil pH as 4.5. That could yield a much deeper blue to violet color.

Hydrangea macrophylla 'David Ramsey'

Rules of the road for acidifying the soil around your hydrangea.

- Water the day before acidifying to ensure the plant is well hydrated. You don't want the fertilizer to "burn" it.

- Apply acidifying products on a cloudy or cool day, never during the heat of the day; again, you don't want to cause any burning.

- Test the pH before applying product. If the pH is high, you can add a soil acidifier like elemental sulfur or iron sulfate to bring it down to the desired level. Aluminum sulfate is a third amendment that you can buy to lower the pH.

A soil acidifier is used for blue hydrangeas

A word of caution: be aware that if you use a high-phosphorous fertilizer to boost flower production, you run the risk of the phosphorous tying up the aluminum, preventing development of blue color in the flowers no matter how much acidifier you apply. Too much phosphorous can take the blue right out of your flowers over time as no aluminum can get to them. No aluminum = no blue. Again, your local garden center can help you find the right product to change the flower colors to blue.

PRUNING *HYDRANGEA MACROPHYLLA* AND *H. SERRATA*: WHY, HOW, AND WHEN

If I told you how many times I get asked about pruning, you would be amazed. I expect it at horticultural gatherings. But it never fails that at all manner of family events and outings with friends, even at the grocery store, this question comes up. So much so, my husband and sisters have witnessed the exchange so often that they can answer it.

Be aware that, in general, if your *Hydrangea macrophylla* and *H. serrata* never came in contact with a pair of pruners or loppers they still would perform well. So, you might ask yourself the more important question at the outset: "Why am I pruning this plant?"

Most *H. macrophyllas* and *H. serratas* bloom on old wood, particularly the older varieties. I can tell you with certainty that if your *Hydrangea macrophylla* or *H. serrata* predates 2004, it is an old-wood bloomer (see page 13), and it's most likely 'Nikko Blue'. How do I know that, you ask? Because 2004 is the year in which Endless Summer®, the first repeat-blooming *Hydrangea macrophylla*, was introduced in the market. After that, many more introductions came on the scene that have the genetic ability to bloom on old and new wood.

The answer to the question of when to prune lies in knowing your plant, including the type of plant you have. Often a gardener has no clue. So you need to go ask yourself a series of other questions to get a best-guess answer to determine which hydrangea you have, and go from there.

You, however, are much more informed than the average person asking a pruning question. I'll try to make the pruning process a little less daunting for you.

Why Prune?

Hydrangeas remain floriferous without ever being pruned as long as they are getting the right cultural conditions. If the hydrangea is too big for the space in which you have planted it, I encourage you to rethink your garden design. Today there are so many options in the marketplace, you can easily replace it with a smaller plant. That would relieve you of the pruning chore (Who needs another task?) and probably restore marital bliss (I'm just guessing here.) You can even donate the plant you dig up to a local garden club for their annual plant sale, your town library, a community center—you get the idea. Everybody wins!

If you are going to prune, there are some general pruning guidelines that apply to hydrangeas as they do to all shrubs. The "3 Ds" is your first order of business.

Remove dead, diseased, and damaged wood as soon as you see it anytime of year. Remove crossing branches as they will lead to bruising and form gateways for insect invasions. Deadhead (remove faded and spent flowers) to neaten up the plant. (When it comes to rebloomers, deadheading actually stimulates flowering; see page15.) Keep in mind that all pruning stimulates plant growth.

Pruning Ground Rules

At the risk of being overly cautious, I want to make sure we're all on the same page, so to speak. Here are some basic pruning ground rules. First, be sure you prune with sharp, disinfected bypass pruners, not anvil pruners.

Second, be manic about garden hygiene. Always disinfect your pruning tools. I like to use Lysol® spray to get into hard-to-reach places like the nooks and crannies of my loppers. I use disinfecting wipes for the blades of my cutters when I'm working on more than one plant. That way there's no spread of diseases from plant to plant. I avoid bleach solutions as they are corrosive if you don't do a good job of rinsing, and you must thoroughly dry the rinsed blades to avoid rust. Too labor intensive for me!

Pruning Tools

BYPASS PRUNERS

Bypass pruners work like scissors in that both edges slip past each other so that you get a nice, clean cut.

Bypass pruners

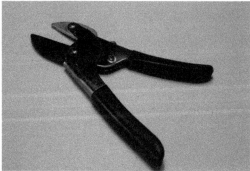
Anvil pruners

ANVIL PRUNERS

Anvil pruners, on the other hand, will crush and sometimes shred a stem as the single sharp blade catches the stem and makes the cut when that blade hits the solid base of the opposing anvil side of the pruner.

Because cuts made with anvil pruners are usually less than "clean," the plant needs to work harder and use precious energy to heal the cut. It's simply better if the plant uses that energy to make flowers and foliage.

LOPPERS

Loppers are simply pruners with long handles.

PRUNING SAW

It's handy to have a pruning saw if you're dealing with larger cuts. This is a small, foldable saw that cuts on the pull stroke.

PRUNING TIMING

The question of when to prune depends on when your plant sets buds for its following bloom season.

Hydrangeas That Bloom on Old Wood

Step one for pruning *Hydrangea macrophylla* and *H. serrata* is the baseline knowledge of whether it blooms on old wood (stems that were grown in previous years) or new wood (stems grown during the current year). Pretty easy, right?

Step two is knowing what this means in hydrangea-land. Some hydrangeas flower on old wood, some flower on new wood, and others flower both on old and new wood.

Step three is knowing the science of when a hydrangea sets its flowerbuds. Old wood stems set their buds when days are short and night temperatures are consistently below 60 degrees. Let's translate that to the calendar. Days start getting shorter in the northern hemisphere sometime on June 21, the summer solstice (attention, old wood hydrangea stems!). In the North, nighttime temps start dropping into the 60s usually sometime in August (later if you live in warmer parts of the country). That's when those old wood stems start forming flowerbuds for the following garden year—talk about planning!

What does that mean for you? If you have a hydrangea that blooms exclusively on old wood like *Hydrangea macrophylla* 'Pia', keep the pruners away from that plant after August 1 to be safe, unless, of course, you're prepared to risk losing some flowers as you continually force the plant into a space that's too small for its ultimate size. Again, those living in warmer zones can prune later than August 1. Keep in mind that all *Hydrangea macrophylla* need a chilling period to initiate bud formation and set those buds, just like daffodils, so don't wait too long to prune once those night temps stay in the 60s.

Hydrangea macrophylla 'Pia'

Deadheading

Deadhead to remove the dead flowerheads; cut stems at a forty-five degree angle one-quarter inch above the first healthy bud on the stem. If you have a rebloomer, the sooner you deadhead, the better to stimulate reblooming. If you don't, it's a matter of taste and how you want your garden to look.

Pruning for Size

After that, you should prune immediately after the plant has flowered using the same cutting technique so you don't affect those new flowerbuds.

The hard part, however, is being able to clearly see what you're doing with all that foliage. What you might do is, in the early spring before the plant has leafed out, go out and put twist ties on stems you want to remove. That way you can be sure it's old wood.

Also mark stems that need to go for some other reason. Then when you go out with the loppers in July, you will already have designated the cuts you'll be making.

The proper way to deadhead is at a 45-degree angle

A pruning cut made above petioles shows the nodes where new growth is already underway

A stem has been marked with white twist tie in late winter for later pruning

Winterkill

If you're looking for dead branches, don't be fooled by those that have brown tips.

A stem in spring with dead tips and live emerging foliage

A *Hydrangea macrophylla* with the tips cut off, whose buds grew further and were blasted by later cold spring weather

Those are simply tips with winterkill, which you can remove—but don't be too quick. Although that tip might be brown and dead, those nascent buds farther down might produce a flower, though it may be a bit later than usual during a cool spring. And removing that tip can stimulate growth in those stems. If bad weather comes before the final seasonal warm-up, that entire branch can be killed back; best to leave it be for a while.

Hold off until you're past the danger zone in your location, and then remove that dead tip. You could even wait until you see flowerbuds emerge from growth beneath the tip before you take your pruners to it.

A *Hydrangea macrophylla* flower emerging from below a dead tip

If you notice branches without plump purple or green leaf buds, they are likely dead, but I suggest you cut them back a little at a time (tip pruning) to test that. If all you see inside is white, brown, or beige tissue, and no green, then it is assuredly dead, and you can cut it down. You may need a hand lens or magnifying glass to see these colors clearly.

One type of hand lens available at retail

You can also use your fingernail to scratch the stem to test for live wood, which will be green.

Then you'll know where the live wood begins to make your cut. When you cut away an entire branch, do it at the base of the shrub.

By the way, some other plants bloom on old wood too. Azaleas, rhododendrons, and forsythias are examples. Ever see a forsythia in the spring that looks like it's missing flowers in large swaths? That's a plant that was pruned too late. Some overenthusiastic gardener probably took a hedge trimmer to it in the fall,

Scratch the stem of *Hydrangea macrophylla* to determine its viability

which resulted in "bald spots." But forsythias have much better stem hardiness than hydrangeas. Those other branches that weren't cut bloomed just fine, even after a deep winter cold blast like the recent polar vortex events. Most roses, on the other hand, bloom on new wood, which is why they are pruned in the spring before they set their buds and flower.

The Importance of Apical Dominance in Pruning

Let's go back to the removal of those dead tips with winterkill. This may actually turn out to be a good thing for repeat bloomers. Now is the time to get into something called "apical dominance."

Apical dominance is the suppression of side (lateral) bud development in a growing plant shoot caused by hormones produced in the tip of the shoot. The plant tip (apical bud) controls this hormone (auxin). Auxin prevents lateral buds from growing so that the plant can use all available energy to grow its apical bud; that is, it has apical dominance. So it is with reblooming hydrangeas. Before it breaks dormancy, a flowerbud at the end of a branch controls the growth of the flowerbuds below it; it has apical dominance in that it controls the growth hormones for the flowers farther down that stem. When that tip bud is removed, the lower buds are released from its "control." Those other flowers are free to fully form and deliver on their promise, unless, of course, they also have been blasted by some weather-related injury.

You can selectively choose to remove any tip you want on a plant that might need tidying up. Your reward will be more flowers. If you are a northern gardener, however, I strongly recommend you refrain from neatening up your *Hydrangea macrophylla* shrubs until after May 15. I have experienced far too many late-season ice storms where a prematurely "spring cleaned" *Hydrangea macrophylla* lost its last chance to flower when it was blasted by a May weather surprise.

Remember, "tip pruning" will not generate more flowers on plants that bloom only on old wood since there are no nascent flower buds sleeping in the stems. That's another vote for reblooming hydrangeas.

Apical dominance is the reason you want to deadhead rebloomers. The sooner you get rid of that spent flower, the sooner auxin will flow to the sleeping bud to produce yet another flower for you. It's the magic of rebloomers!

You might come across branch tips that have "mummies," which are flowerbuds from the previous season that never opened and which eventually froze on the plant.

Even the usually dependable rebloomers can sometimes let you down. But mummies aren't a lost cause. Knowing what you learned about apical dominance, think of mummies as opportunities to get that second bloom earlier. After all danger of frost and late storms have passed, you can fearlessly cut them off to release those powerful auxins, put down fertilizer, and accelerate the timetable for the plant's second flush of flowers. With warmer extended summers, a little TLC, and some extra irrigation, you may enjoy that second flush of flowers sooner rather than later.

A *Hydrangea macrophylla* mummy

The photo to the right shows what a reblooming hydrangea looked like one June when winter had killed all the tips. They were completely removed to release the full power of the auxins to the lateral buds for the most flower power the plant could produce that summer.

Hydrangea macrophylla after tip pruning to encourage reblooming

Hydrangeas That Bloom on Old and New Wood

What if your hydrangea is one that blooms on old and new wood? Ah, the plot thickens. The old wood rule still applies. That plant has old-wood buds on it that were made after August 1 of last year, just waiting to show themselves. But let's say that plant has already bloomed earlier in the season. Now what? Again, you can make your cuts right after blooming as that will, in fact, encourage more growth on that rebloomer before the season ends. Or, you can leave everything alone. The plant will still pump out flowers on the new stems it has been making all season, assuming you have been treating it well.

Gardeners who live in zones colder than 6 (like Michigan) and grow rebloomers typically cut them down in the spring. They get their only flower flush on that new wood production later in the season.

Clearly, if summer storms take out a stem or two from any of your hydrangeas—old wood or new wood—remove them to tidy up the plant. Then, just sit back and enjoy the show!

That's a lot of information about hydrangea pruning, the biggest mystery of our time. Here's a summary:

A CHECKLIST FOR *HYDRANGEA MACROPHYLLA* AND *H. SERRATA* PRUNING

Ask yourself these questions before pruning *H. macrophylla* and *H. serrata*.

1. Why prune at all? Should the plant be moved to a different (better) spot? Should it be replaced with a plant that won't ever need to be pruned?

2. If you must prune it, determine if it blooms on old wood, new wood, or both. Then follow the guidance for old wood and new wood.

3. Look at the calendar. If the plant blooms at all on old wood, and it has just bloomed, now is the time to take the shears to it, if at all. If it is after August 1*, be prepared to risk losing next year's flowers if you do any cutting now.

4. Look at the plant. If it is four years old or older, and if it looks "tired" after it has just bloomed, it may actually need to be pruned to rejuvenate it (a rare occurrence). In that case, remove one-third of the oldest canes by cutting them down to the ground immediately after the plant ceases blooming so it can generate new growth in time to set flowers and harden-off for the winter.

5. If it blooms on old wood and new wood, follow the old wood rules if you want flowers in early summer.

Unless you live in zones 7, 8, 9 where you could take a chance and wait a little longer.

THE FUTURE OF *HYDRANGEA MACROPHYLLA*

Hydrangea macrophylla is the species that has the most cultivars in the market and the species that has the most ongoing work in breeding, testing, and production. There are two main reasons for this: one is its enormous popularity; it's simply a showstopper with a buying public that seems insatiable. The second is its sensitivity to cold temperatures.

Flower production continues to be an issue in cold areas, as roots are hardy to zone 4 (in some cases) with stems that are not, disappointing gardeners many a summer, leaving them without early-season flowers. Reblooming cultivars have given those gardeners the opportunity to enjoy flowers later in the season if the summer is a warm one, which has been the case the past few years, owing to climate change.

If breeders can come up with a *Hydrangea macrophylla* with better stem hardiness, then that will rejuvenate a market of hydrangea-hungry gardeners, myself among them. *Ka-ching!*

Hydrangea serrata 'Bluebird'

Hydrangea serrata
MOUNTAIN HYDRANGEA

Hydrangea serrata is often sold in the marketplace as *Hydrangea macrophylla* and is confused by many as being the same plant, but it is not. Debate continues about whether or not it should be a separate species but, as of now, the decision has been made to keep it as a subspecies of *Hydrangea macrophylla*. It is, however, important to make this distinction because *Hydrangea serrata* has a lot going for it that will serve northern gardeners very well in the breeding of cold-hardy cultivars. Let's get to the facts.

It's easy to see why this plant is often confused with *Hydrangea macrophylla*. It shares the same flower forms, both mophead and lacecap. It has the same characteristic propensity to pH sensitivity, changing color when lime or acidic amendments are added to the soil (as discussed for *Hydrangea macrophylla*). It's extremely tolerant of salty air, so shoreline communities enjoy its beauty.

Hydrangea serrata 'Preziosa'

Where *Hydrangea serratas* are markedly different from their *Hydrangea macrophylla* cousins is in their size and hardiness. First, *Hydrangea serrata* hails from the mountains of Japan, where plants have endured centuries of colder temperatures, which in turn has led to a better cold tolerance. They carry the common name "mountain hydrangea" as a result of that bloodline. That bloodline makes them more likely than *Hydrangea macrophylla* to withstand colder temperatures and produce flowers.

You might also be able to distinguish *Hydrangea serrata* by the sometimes-reddish tint to the foliage. Many of them turn red in the fall, adding to your autumnal color display.

Hydrangea serrata 'Blue Billow' with a hint of red in its foliage

Until recently, *Hydrangea serratas* were also generally smaller plants than *Hydrangea macrophyllas*, maxing out at 4 feet by 4 feet with flowers the size of baseballs rather than melons. But newer cultivars of *Hydrangea macrophylla* are now even smaller so that size differentiation is no longer so distinct.

A great advantage of newer and smaller *Hydrangea serratas* is that they are rebloomers. Additionally, they are better able to hide under a lighter blanket of snow (and thus get better winter protection) than a larger specimen, which might poke way up to be exposed to wintry winds and colder seasonal blasts. Some of the newer market introductions have come in at a mere eighteen inches and fit very nicely into a perennial border.

Hydrangea serrata 'Blue Billow' when it first colors

WHY WON'T MY HYDRANGEAS BLOOM?

Now we get to your *real* question. I know, I know. This is what you have wanted to know all along, but I couldn't delve into this until we crawled through the first few sections. You see, all of this information fits together like a giant jigsaw puzzle and forms the foundation you needed to get to this point. In fact, you already know the answer to this question by virtue of the preceding pages, but let me sum it up for you.

Hydrangeas that bloom on old wood (and you know which ones fit that definition) flower unreliably because of what we haven't done right, in terms of care, or because of the hand Mother Nature has dealt us. Here are some examples:

Cultural Issues

Cultural issues have to do with care, which gardeners can control. Here are some cultural mistakes that can cause hydrangeas not to bloom or to bloom unreliably:

Problem: Untimely pruning. You pruned a plant that blooms on old wood during the spring, late fall, or winter after it set its flowerbuds, effectively cutting off those buds.

Solution: Just take care of the 3 Ds, then walk away!

Problem: Plants are not getting enough sun.

Solution: Move the plants. Don't be fooled; all *Hydrangea macrophyllas* and *H. serratas* need some sun.

Problem: The plant has lots of beautiful green leaves but no flowers.

Solution: Cut down on applying nitrogen fertilizer and water. Plants will always make leaves over flowers if they get too much of either. Finding that right balance is the key.

Weather

Here's why plants affected by weather might not be blooming.

Late fall cold snaps: The buds that formed after August 1 froze or dried out before the plant was able to go fully dormant and harden off.

Deep winter cold: Those vexing bouts with the polar vortex, other deep winter cold, or icy winds killed the buds.

Late spring cold: Plants made it through all other winter challenges and broke dormancy only to be hit by a late spring storm that killed its flowerbuds (*Mon Dieu!*).

Weather isn't something we can do much about unless your plant is in a container. Then you can move it out of the weather into a protected space or even into a greenhouse, if you're lucky enough to have such a luxury.

However, many gardeners have found that if they take some extra steps to winter protect their in-ground plants, they have better luck in some seasons and/or geographies.

HOW TO PROTECT PLANTS DURING THE WINTER

- Use wind breaks to block icy winter winds to prevent desiccation of tender flowerbuds. This can be a building or a temporary structure you devise for the winter. Do whatever works where your plant is sited.

- Try to plant hydrangeas under the shelter of trees with winter-persistent foliage such as conifers, oaks, and beeches.

- Insulate plants using chicken wire or tomato cages filled with leaves, straw, and other lightweight materials. Remember to remove this insulation after all danger of frost has passed, and do it carefully on a cloudy or cool day to avoid damaging the tender buds, which may already have broken dormancy.

There are gardeners as far north as Ontario, Canada, who wrap their plants in plastic leaf bags and loosely fill those bags with leaves for the winter who have great success.

Hydrangeas wrapped in plastic bags stuffed with leaves protected for winter

ONE SOLUTION: BREAK FREE FROM OLD-WOOD BLOOMERS

If all of this old-wood blooming angst is just too much for you, break free! Consider moving/donating/replacing those purely old-wood bloomers and trade up to the newer reblooming cultivars. Or consider *H. serrata*, which is much more cold hardy.

An old-wood blooming lacecap called 'Lady in Red' is extremely cold hardy. Despite all of the cold climate challenges I have experienced over the past ten years in zone 5B, she has never failed to flower for me.

In an ideal world, I would simply provide a list of preferable hydrangeas on a spreadsheet so you could source plants based on the colors you want, or maybe the size you want, or some other criteria. Sadly, or maybe not so sadly, that's an impossible task.

Each year and in each hardiness zone, a dizzying array of new *Hydrangea macrophylla* and *Hydrangea serrata* options are presented to consumers. Often with these new introductions, labels are missing key data or the garden center staff have gaps in their information. To make the choices even harder, plants are put out for sale when they are blooming their heads off and they are screaming, "Buy me, buy me!"—so plant lust takes over the gardener.

Hydrangea serrata 'Preziosa'

Additionally, the plants show up at the grocery store, hardware store, box stores—it seems they are just everywhere! Impossible to resist!

What can you do to stave off this attack of plant lust when you are ambushed like this while at the same time deciphering the labels or catalog descriptions as their siren calls distract you, so that you can make the best selection possible?

If you live in a zone where your old-wood bloomers have failed more often than not, then I strongly suggest you limit your purchases to plants that have reblooming capability. Why settle for a green bush when you can have wowie zowie flowers and colors *and* a green bush?

If the plant tag doesn't say outright that it's a rebloomer, you can usually decode it from the label or description. Look for words like "repeat blooms" or whether the bloom key shows it flowering in June, July, August, and September. You might even see the words "everblooming" or "free flowering," both of which are used to refer to hydrangeas that are rebloomers. The last option is to search the internet and simply look the plant up, specifically querying "rebloomer." That should give you the info you need to make a purchase. Then have the courage to walk away if it's not a rebloomer.

Worst case, buy the plant you're lusting after and consider it an annual. You'll get more out of a plant that flowers this season than you will from a bouquet of fresh flowers that die in a matter of ten to fourteen days, right? I think you're already ahead on that deal.

A word of caution: not all rebloomers are created equal. I have trialed many in my garden that did not fulfill their promise despite giving them the right growing conditions. By the time they got around to putting out a second flush of flowers, the season had closed, and I was left with lots of "mummies," buds that never opened and eventually froze on the plant.

My advice to you is to identify the rebloomers that work best in your area by getting input from other local gardeners or reputable independent garden centers. Then make that purchase.

Hydrangea macrophylla Cityline® Paris blooms on old wood

ONE LAST POINT OF INFORMATION FOR YOU

Let me tell you what hydrangea growers and breeders know. In very general terms, *Hydrangea macrophylla* and *H. serrata* old-wood flowers are induced through a period of 6 weeks of temperatures below 60 degrees F when the buds set, followed by a dormant period of 6 weeks of temperatures between 35 degrees F to 45 degrees F. Growers typically then raise temps for approximately 80 days to bring on flowers in time for gift plants for events such as Easter and Mother's Day. Growers follow the same process to force flowers for flower shows and other events. Keep this in mind whenever you consider pruning your plants or question why they aren't flowering. Isn't science great?

THE FUTURE OF *HYDRANGEA SERRATA*

Hydrangea serrata has great promise for northern gardeners who are hoping for more cold hardiness. It already has a leg up owing to its Japanese mountain heritage, which has been harnessed for breeding programs, and it is rumored to be frequently studied for more. I, for one, am glad to have this little beauty poking its nose around. Bring it on!

Hydrangea quercifolia
OAKLEAF HYDRANGEA

Oakleaf hydrangeas are native to the southeastern U.S., mostly in woodland settings from zones 5 to 9. Their stupendous foliage, flowers, and multiple seasons of interest have made this a popular garden plant up and down the East Coast as well as farther inland. Add to that its easy-care nature and you have a handsome, first-class plant.

The interesting foliage resembles oak leaves, hence the name.

Its flower provides a long season of color without demanding full sun. A winning feature is the deep wine color the leaves acquire as the temperatures cool.

Hydrangea quercifolia leaves

Its exfoliating winter bark is nothing to sneeze at as you gaze at a somewhat dull winter landscape, giving the plant true four-season interest.

This plant's tolerance for drought once it's established is yet another reason, in addition to its year-round interest, to find room for it somewhere in your garden. What's not to like?

Hydrangea quercifolia fall foliage color

It used to be that oak leaf hydrangeas only came in giant sizes of 6 to 8 feet high and wide, or larger. But all of that has changed; today's marketplace is overflowing with many smaller options. Newer cultivars are introduced each season at two-thirds its original size and smaller. Some new introductions even have chartreuse-colored foliage that create exciting contrast and provide a backdrop for other garden plants—yet another outstanding feature.

Hydrangea quercifolia 'Alice'

The flower form of an oakleaf hydrangea is the panicle: a pointy, cone-shaped beauty that can be 12 to 14 inches in length (or shorter in some specimens).

It can be the beautiful, single-petaled form like 'Alice' or a double flower form as seen on the stupendous specimen 'Snowflake'.

You will be equally wowed by recent introductions with star-shaped florets and densely packed flowerheads, which can light up your garden like beacons.

The flowers can be impressively large. On all varieties, they start white or cream and age to shades of pink and rose. Because the flowers open from the bottom, you'll often get a two-toned effect as they develop and mature.

Hydrangea quercifolia Snowflake™

Hydrangea quercifolia 'Little Honey'

You can't manipulate the color of this flower regardless of soil pH. The depth of rose color that develops depends on the genetics of the individual plants or cultivars.

WHERE TO PLANT YOUR *HYDRANGEA QUERCIFOLIA*

Hydrangea quercifolia is mainly an understory plant so my best advice is to plant it at the edge of a shade garden or somewhere it can get morning sun. Think of your *Hydrangea quercifolia* as a woodland plant. It will do well with dappled light, mulched with shredded leaves or bark. The farther north you garden, the more sun you can give it. Not so in southern gardens, where it must be shaded

Hydrangea quercifolia Jetstream™

in the afternoon. Additionally, because this hydrangea is an old-wood bloomer, you need to give those nascent buds some winter protection.

Hot, dry, exposed sites spell certain death for this plant. It needs moist but well-drained soil and is one of the few hydrangeas that abhors constantly wet conditions, which cause the roots to rot.

In its natural setting, the base of a *Hydrangea quercifolia* would be covered with fallen forest leaves and other organic matter so be sure to mimic that environment and provide similar mulching material.

PRUNING YOUR *HYDRANGEA QUERCIFOLIA*

Oakleaf hydrangeas bloom on old wood although breeders are working on reblooming cultivars. Consistent with our discussion about old wood/new wood, you generally shouldn't be cutting this plant after about August 1 unless you're prepared to forfeit some flowers next year.

Remember to take care of the 3 Ds whenever you see them: dead, damaged, and diseased wood. Remove any of it as soon as you see it at any time of year, especially after storms. Keep in mind that all pruning results in a growth response. After taking care of the 3 Ds, you shouldn't be cutting your plant at all, so get that "Do Not Prune" sign ready or send your head pruner on a fishing trip.

If the plant is outgrowing its space, consider moving it to the right-sized place or donating it to someone who has that right-sized space. Replace it with another of the many choices on the market that will fit better in the space you have and make your garden positively sing once it's established.

Oakleaf hydrangeas don't need pruning cuts to encourage flowering; they do that on their own.

One last note about *Hydrangea quercifolias*. Be heartened in the knowledge that old-wood blooming *Hydrangea quercifolias* have better stem hardiness than old-wood blooming *Hydrangea macrophyllas*. In a summer when *Hydrangea macrophyllas* might lose their flowers to cold temperatures, *Hydrangea quercifolias* might well pass them by to still produce their flowers regardless of those same cold temperatures.

Hydrangea petiolaris
CLIMBING HYDRANGEA

If you are looking for a bulletproof vine that absolutely laughs at all manner of challenges, this is it. Coming to us from the woodlands of Japan, this vigorous, shade-tolerant climber clings via aerial rootlets and will not harm structures as it makes its way up chimneys, side walls, or even trees.

Hydrangea petiolaris rootlets on an arbor

Once established, *Hydrangea petiolaris* produces a fragrant, cream-colored lacecap flower that stays on the vine throughout the season until you remove it or it falls off on its own.

Climbing hydrangeas typically take about three to five years before they bloom unless the one you buy is already flowering. But even then, your plant might take a break while it puts its energy into getting established. However, once it gets going, stand back and enjoy the show.

One of the most attractive features of *Hydrangea petiolaris* is its exfoliating bark. As it matures, the main trunk and stems develop a characteristic cinnamon coloration that provides some winter interest, so siting your vine where it can be enjoyed in the off season may be a consideration.

This is a sprawling and woody vine, sometimes growing into a mound at its base, or an attractive groundcover. Because of its vigor, it needs a strong support structure if grown vertically. About the only place it will not grow is in extreme cold or heat, as it is rated for hardiness zones 4 through 8.

Hydrangea petiolaris growing over a stump

WHERE TO PLANT YOUR *HYDRANGEA PETIOLARIS*

This plant does well in part to full shade but it can also tolerate full sun with enough moisture; north-facing walls or structures are ideal. Try to select a climbing area or structure that won't need painting or maintenance so that you won't have to dislodge the vine once it has begun to climb.

The soil should be rich, fertile, and moist but well drained. Climbing hydrangea doesn't do well in very hot southern climates, but those geographies offer an abundance of other flashy and fragrant vine choices.

If you have a tree stump you wish to hide, this plant will scamper over it and engulf it with foliage in no time.

You'll be able to camouflage just about any unsightly garden eyesore.

HYDRANGEA PETIOLARIS FLOWERS

Hydrangea petiolaris blooms on old wood producing creamy white, delightfully fragrant lacecap flowers. Don't expect to change the flower color; the flower starts out a creamy white and stays that way. There might be a slight color change as the flower ages but, as of the date of this publication, I can say with certainty that it does not respond to changes in pH.

The lacecap flower of *Hydrangea petiolaris*

The good news is that you now have several options for color in the foliage of your climbing hydrangea. There are newer introductions, including 'Firefly' and 'Kuga Variegata', with variegated foliage that might be of interest. However, the downside is that these variegated versions are shy when it comes to flowering. Plant these for their attention-grabbing foliage.

One added note: Deer have never touched this plant in my garden regardless of the season or its location. I won't go so far as to call it deer-proof, but it has turned out to be extremely deer-resistant, right up there with lavender, lambs' ears, sage, and some others. Woo-hoo!

Hydrangea petiolaris 'Firefly'

PRUNING YOUR *HYDRANGEA PETIOLARIS*

When it comes to pruning, climbing hydrangeas bloom on old wood, plain and simple. Don't prune after August 1 unless you want to sacrifice some of next year's blooms. If you must cut it to keep it in shape for some reason, do it right after it has flowered. However, I encourage you not to cut your plant at all unless it has been damaged in a storm and needs to be cleaned up.

Climbing hydrangeas don't need your pruning cuts to encourage flowering; they do that on their own as long as you provide the right cultural conditions for them. Be confident that those old-wood stems are much more winter hardy than the other old-wood hydrangeas. Mine has never failed to produce flowers over the course of the twenty years I have had it in multiple sites throughout my zone 5B garden. I put this plant in the category of garden-worthy workhorses.

Hydrangea petiolaris growing over an arbor

Hydrangea arborescens
SMOOTH, WOODLAND HYDRANGEA

We may as well call this hydrangea "old reliable." It's native to woodlands in the eastern United States and has been in gardens since the early 20th century when it was first introduced as a passalong plant from rural Illinois.

It has a lot going for it. There is no amount of deer browse, overzealous late fall pruning, or winter kill that will deter it from giving you magnificent early-summer flowers.

You're probably most familiar with the specimen 'Annabelle', which has billowy white flowers. They always start greenish white in early summer before turning pure white and then back to green on the tips of the stems. Those stems can sometimes be soft and weak, causing the flowers to flop. That can be avoided with some judicious pruning at the right time.

Although 'Annabelle' is a carefree and dependable, medium-sized, deciduous shrub that laughs at cold temperatures (hardy to zone 4), some of the newer cultivars on the market are even tougher and are hardy to zone 3. *Hydrangea arborescens* can even take the heat to zone 9 as long as you give it shade.

This hydrangea is also a spreader. Your initial plant will grow in width as it suckers along the ground. That's actually a good thing, as you can easily make more plants to plant elsewhere simply by digging up outlying suckers from the colony.

Hydrangea arborescens 'Annabelle'

Hydrangea arborescens is an important wildlife food source. At my home, we often observe our local bird population feeding on the spent flowerheads right through the winter, so don't be too hasty to deadhead this one to tidy it up. If you leave it alone, not only will you have winter interest and winter food for birds, but you may very well have "volunteer" plants pop up in your garden from time to time. *Hydrangea arborescens* flowers have both male and female organs and, when pollinated by bees, the fertile seeds can produce new plants, a delightful surprise and just about the easiest propagation technique I know.

You're most likely to find the snowball-like flower form of this plant offered for sale but in the wild you'll sometimes see a less common lacecap flower form. A few newer cultivars on the market have lacecap flowers. The lacecaps are fragrant. Look for the wild ones the next time you find yourself hiking in the late spring/early summer; it's a real treat to see and smell them.

Hydrangea arborescens subspecies 'Radiata'

WHERE TO PLANT YOUR *HYDRANGEA ARBORESCENS*

The fact that *Hydrangea arborescens* is native to the eastern United States tells you that it's an easy-to-grow plant as most natives are well adapted to whatever Mother Nature throws at them. It tolerates a fair amount of shade but will produce more flowers in the North when given more sun. Morning sun is best. It will not do well in extremely dry conditions but it will grow in just about any well-drained soil. Rich, humusy conditions are ideal so think about replicating the conditions found on the forest floor and you'll have hit the nail on the head. Severe winters may kill off the top growth but it will usually regenerate and bloom its head off for you. Its egg-shaped, toothed foliage even provides some color as it turns butter yellow in the fall, so site it somewhere you can use that to your advantage.

HYDRANGEA ARBORESCENS FLOWERS

There's no chance of changing the flower color of a *Hydrangea arborescens*. The color might change as the flower ages but as of the date of this publication, I can say with certainty that it's not possible to manipulate the color of the flower. Some start out green, turn white and back to green; others start out deep rose, fade to a lighter pink; and so on. The plant label will tell you what to expect about flower color.

The good news is that you now have several flower color options when you go to the garden center or peruse the garden catalogs. Since 'Annabelle' was introduced, breeders have come up with reblooming cultivars and choices of flower colors ranging from green to white to light pink to deep rose.

Along with those new color options have come stupendous flowers, stronger stems, and choices of plants smaller in size than 'Annabelle'. If your garden cannot accommodate her hefty 5 feet by 5 feet mature size or you don't want to sign up for an annual pruning job of such magnitude, now you don't have to. Let's hear it for progress!

Hydrangea arborescens Invincibelle® Spirit II flower

PRUNING YOUR *HYDRANGEA ARBORESCENS*

General pruning guidelines apply to *Hydrangea arborescens* as previously covered for other hydrangeas. Take care of the 3 Ds first: dead, damaged, and diseased wood. Remove any of it as soon as you see it anytime of year. Crossing branches should also be removed, as they will lead to bruising of the plant and form gateways for insect invasions.

All *Hydrangea arborescens* bloom on new wood, which makes your pruning decisions relatively easy. What that translates to is that the current season's flowers develop at the tips of the branches that are grown during the current season. What that means is that you could get a head start and prune your new wood bloomers in the fall, winter, or early spring.

But—and this is a big "but"—unless you garden in a somewhat benign warm climate, I advise against pruning your new-wood bloomers in the fall. Remember that pruning does three things: first it wounds the plant and the plant will try to heal itself. Second, that wound is a gateway for pests, although fewer of them are around late in the season. Third, pruning stimulates the plant to grow and in the fall, you want plants to "quiet down" and go into dormancy. Pruning is not the right message to be sending it.

What you risk with fall pruning is slower healing, potential pest invasion, and essentially less winter protection for those stems you really want to keep healthy farther down on the plant. Why risk all of that for the sake of a day or two? That being said, here is general guidance for pruning *Hydrangea arborescens*.

Hydrangea arborescens can be pruned "hard" down to about 18 inches in fall, winter, or early spring. Regardless of when you prune it, the pruning response you will get from that treatment will be brand-new, weak, thin stems that might not be able to hold the large flowers.

Hydrangea arborescens spring growth after being pruned to a height of 18 inches

A better idea is simply to deadhead the plant. This will allow the mature stems to get stronger and be better able to hold the new flowers. You can also cut the stems in half or remove one-third of each stem to rejuvenate the plant, which will also keep the stems strong and the plant healthy.

Hydrangea arborescens Invincibelle® Spirit II post-pruning   *Hydrangea arborescens* Incrediball® in winter

If you're interested in providing food for wildlife and having some winter interest in your landscape, leave the flowerheads until spring for the birds. If you wait until then, make sure you stop cutting in time to let the flowerbuds form for the current year.

THE FUTURE OF *HYDRANGEA ARBORESCENS*

The future of *Hydrangea arborescens* looks rosy indeed. The sheer dependability of the plant based on its zone hardiness and new-wood blooming strength already supports its popularity. Recent successes of new cultivars like Incrediball® and Invincibelle® Spirit have put smiles on the faces of retailers and consumers alike, guaranteeing better versions of this garden staple. Diminutive sizes are already in the marketplace, and I can guess that greater variety in foliage and flowers is not far behind.

Hydrangea paniculata Diamond Rouge®

Hydrangea paniculata
PANICLE, PEE GEE

Native to southern and eastern Asia, this hydrangea gets its name from its flower form, a showy, cone-shaped, tapered panicle made up of many tiny florets. You might be more familiar with the name "Pee Gee hydrangea," the common reference for *paniculata* 'Grandiflora', which in Latin translates loosely to "large panicle flower."

Hydrangea paniculata 'Limelight'

Many *Hydrangea paniculatas* are cold hardy down to zone 3, a zone in which other hydrangeas would literally freeze to death. Their best feature is that they bloom on new wood, making them foolproof, regardless of overenthusiastic pruning, deer browse, and finicky weather. Unfortunately, you will have a very hard time growing them in zones warmer than 7, where they will just cook. But then there are many other flowering plants that can take their place in those heat zones.

You can get *Hydrangea paniculata* in a traditional shrub form or as a topiary, sold as a "standard" or what I like to refer to as a "lollipop." Both have their place in a garden as colorful, versatile, low-maintenance shrubs. Some can begin flowering as early as June in warm seasons in northern gardens and even earlier in warmer climates. They will continue flowering right through the summer, some on strong stems that hold the flowers well until frost takes its toll. As garden-worthy plants, several have earned awards in a variety of competitions around the world.

Hydrangea paniculata trained as a young standard

WHERE TO PLANT YOUR *HYDRANGEA PANICULATA*

You don't need an exceptionally large space for one of these beauties: *H. paniculatas* can range in size from a diminutive 24 inches tall to a towering 8 feet or more when they are happy. Select one that fits your space.

If you are lamenting the fact that you don't have enough shade to grow *Hydrangea macrophylla* or *Hydrangea quercifolia* successfully, weep no more. This is the plant for you. *Hydrangea paniculata* loves sun. In many cases, the more you give it, the happier it is. That's not to say that you can't provide a little shade.

In fact, if you garden in the South, you will have no choice but to give it some relief from the sun.

Generally, though, they perform best and are the most floriferous in full sun to part shade in moist, organically rich, well-drained soil. Once they are established, they are somewhat drought-tolerant, but they won't be happy in either extremely dry, exposed sites and or constantly wet conditions.

HYDRANGEA PANICULATA FLOWERS

As with *Hydrangea arborescens*, you won't be able to manipulate the flower colors of *Hydrangea paniculata*. The color will change as the flower ages the way it does on *Hydrangea quercifolia*, but as of the date of this publication, I can say with certainty that it's not possible to change the color of the flower.

Like *Hydrangea quercifolia*, the flower form of a *Hydrangea paniculata* is the panicle: a pointy, cone-shaped stunner 12 to 16 inches long (or shorter in some specimens). It develops at the end of the stems. For now, *Hydrangea paniculata* exists only in the single-petalled form, but one of the more interesting recent introductions is a panicle consisting of large, star-shaped florets on a plant with arching stems.

Hydrangea paniculata Great Star™

The panicle flower can be quite large. It starts white and ages to shades of pink, rose, and even strawberry red and burgundy in some cases. The flowers open from the bottom of the inflorescence upward so you'll often see a multitoned effect as the flowers develop.

The flower type can vary in size and quantity by cultivar. The tighter cone-shaped flowers are probably the ones with which you're most familiar and that are shown in the photos thus far in this

Hydrangea paniculata Pinky Winky®

book. But you can also get plants with a lacecap look to the flower, such as *Hydrangea paniculata* 'Angel's Blush', which has a more open cone shape similar

to a lacecap form of *Hydrangea macrophylla* (tight florets interspersed with open panicles). This type of flower will attract more pollinators than other *Hydrangea paniculata* types because of the preponderance of open florets. Both are showstoppers.

Flowers aren't your only source of color on today's *Hydrangea paniculata*. Recent cultivars such as *Hydrangea paniculata* 'Yuki Ghessho' offer colored stems and variegated foliage.

Hydrangea paniculata 'Angel's Blush'

Hydrangea paniculata 'Yuki Ghessho'

Hydrangea paniculata 'Fire and Ice' in fall color

Some even offer a deep burgundy flower color once the temperatures cool.

PRUNING YOUR *HYDRANGEA PANICULATA*

General pruning guidelines apply to *Hydrangea paniculatas* as previously covered for other hydrangeas. Take care of the 3 Ds first: dead, damaged, and diseased wood. Remove any of it as soon as you see it anytime of year. Crossing branches should also be removed as they will lead to bruising of the plant and form gateways for insect invasions.

Old-Wood and New-Wood Types

All *Hydrangea paniculatas* bloom on new wood, meaning this season's flowers will develop at the tips of the branches that are grown this year. The pruning timing is slightly different for this one since it blooms later in the summer. Yes, it is a new-wood bloomer and you prune during its dormant period.

Hydrangea paniculata can be pruned in fall, winter, or early spring. You can simply deadhead the plant. Or you can also cut the stems in half and/or remove one-third of each stem to open up the plant, which will also keep the stems strong and the plant healthy.

If you're interested in having some winter interest in your landscape, leave those flowerheads until spring. If you wait until then, stop cutting in time to let the flowerbuds form for the current year. In the worst case scenario, if you just don't get around to deadheading and the new flowers just come, all you need to do is run out and deadhead the plant to neaten it up at the last minute to get it looking its best at just the right time!

Hydrangea paniculata Mystical Flame® flowering without being deadheaded

HYDRANGEA PANICULATA PRUNING LESSONS FROM THE U.K.

Our garden buddies in the United Kingdom did us a great favor and conducted a three-year study in 2004 of forty-seven *Hydrangea paniculata* cultivars. For this study, they planted three of each cultivar in full sun, fed them only to eliminate nutrient deficiencies, and irrigated them only under drought conditions. The best part is they pruned the trial plants three different ways: one was a hard pruning down to two buds (about a foot off the ground); another method was to prune down to four buds (about two feet up); and the third technique was simply to deadhead the plant—they cut no farther down on the stems or shoots.

The results published in 2008 earned several plants the prestigious Royal Horticultural Society's (RHS) Award of Garden Merit for their performances across the board. More importantly for our discussion here, there were several lessons learned about the various pruning approaches.

With some cultivars, the harder the plant was pruned, the stronger the stems developed for the new season. In other cases, it made little or no difference. When plants did respond to pruning, the lightly pruned plants flowered first and had more but smaller flowers than those that were hard pruned. The hard-pruned plants were more vigorous but that vigor sometimes resulted in flowers that were too big for their stems to support and that hard pruning sometimes resulted in delayed flowering.

Hydrangea paniculata Vanilla Strawberry™ shows its initial change from white to pink before deepening to raspberry

From that UK trial one can conclude the following:

- The least amount of pruning yields a bushy shrub with many smaller flowers.

- For a more erect shrub with fewer, larger flowers, prune more severely.

- Remove the weak, small branches and keep only the main leaders to provide the plant's structure.

- *But,* be careful not to create the dreaded weak stems; after pruning, the plant should have fewer strong main stems (leaders) that end as a single main stub.

Hydrangea paniculata Quick Fire® after pruning

HYDRANGEA PANICULATA PRUNING LESSONS FROM THE U.S.

Closer to home, the Chicago Botanic Garden (CBG) conducted a longitudinal study of *Hydrangea paniculata*. Over the course of twelve years, they studied twenty-five cultivars in their preferred site of moist, well-drained soil in full sun. The plants were rated on ornamental qualities, cultural adaptability, winter hardiness, and disease- and pest-resistance. Each shrub was evaluated for a minimum of six years in CBG's zone 5B gardens. At the end of the trial period, plants were rated based on their overall performance against the stated criteria. The test results were published in *Fine Gardening*.

The CBG trial came to different pruning conclusions than the UK trial. The U.S. trial, simply stated, indicates pruning doesn't affect bloom. Their results did not support the belief that annual pruning led to long, weak stems with the exception of one cultivar, 'Dolly'. Of course, CBG had different plants in their trial and their climate was markedly different than that of the UK trials.

See the Resources section on page 159 to find weblinks to download both the RHS report and the CBG study for specific details by plant. If your plant isn't one of the ones mentioned (alas, time marches on), the only way to know about your specific plant is to talk with other gardeners in your area or conduct your own little trial and see what happens. Or not.

I deeply trust both sources and have been doing my own experimentation to see what does and doesn't work, and I've concluded they are both right. That just reinforces what we already know and that is:

ALL GARDENING IS LOCAL (I wish I knew who first said that!)

There is another study underway as I write this book. Rutgers Gardens in New Brunswick, New Jersey, is in the fourth year of a longitudinal trial of twenty-six *Hydrangea paniculatas*. It is too soon to make major conclusions but early assessments point to the need to monitor moisture on *H. paniculata* during times of extreme drought. Plants maintain their viability but flower color and time of bloom seem to be negatively affected. This possible conclusion is consistent with my personal, nonscientific findings from the last two seasons during which my region experienced extended periods of official extreme drought. We should know more in 2018 when the study is concluded.

THE FUTURE OF *HYDRANGEA PANICULATA*

Hydrangea paniculata holds more growth potential for cold climate gardeners who are limited by climatic conditions and are turning to *Hydrangea paniculata* to answer their later season needs. It's hard to argue with a plant that blooms on new wood for most of the summer and is hardy to zone 3. The newer introductions are smaller and more floriferous, with deeper rose-colored flowers, stems, and foliage. We even have cultivars now with flowers that turn a deep wine color in fall as the temperatures fall.

Admittedly, too many introductions of *Hydrangea paniculata* in too short a time created some confusion in the marketplace, which may be why the Chicago Botanic Garden and Rutgers University started trial programs. It was clear that consumers needed some help deciphering choices at the retail level. Be that as it may, this species in all its forms is foolproof, meaning that rebloomers, more variety of flower and foliage colors, and anything else breeders can come up with will have a ready market.

Hydrangea Double Delights™ Wedding Gown displays its unusual modified lacecap flower form.

PART TWO:
GIVING HYDRANGEAS THE BEST CARE

BEAUTIFUL BLOOMS AND HEALTHY PLANTS START WITH GOOD CARE. HERE'S HOW TO FERTILIZE, WATER, MULCH, AND TRANSPLANT FOR GREAT-LOOKING HYDRANGEAS. YOU'LL SEE THAT THESE GUIDELINES ARE GENERALLY THE SAME REGARDLESS OF THE TYPE OF HYDRANGEA YOU HAVE.

Hydrangea paniculata 'Limelight' in garden setting

CHAPTER TWO

FERTILIZING YOUR HYDRANGEAS: WHAT'S THE RIGHT FORMULA?

General Guidance for All Hydrangeas

Fertilizer is primarily made up of three nutrients: Nitrogen (N), Phosphorous (P), and Potassium (K) (sometimes called potash). The percentage of each is noted on the fertilizer label in NPK order. Fertilizer will have different effects, depending on the proportions of each component. Nitrogen, for example, is necessary for leafy green growth and moves quickly through the soil. You will find that lawn fertilizers are high in this nutrient. Phosphorous helps with healthy roots and bloom and seed set, though it takes time for soil microorganisms to integrate phosphorus thoroughly into the soil. More phosphorous usually means more fruit and flowers. Fertilizers labeled as "bloom boosters" will usually have a disproportionately high middle number, for phosphorous. Potassium is for overall health and disease resistance. Like phosphorous, potassium takes its time to be absorbed into your soil and plants. Often there are other ingredients in the fertilizer in small amounts (trace minerals or micronutrients), such as calcium or manganese, which also serve a purpose in plant growth.

START WITH A SOIL SAMPLE

Before you fertilize, take a soil sample and find out exactly what's going on where your hydrangea is planted. That way you can tailor fertilizer applications to the specific needs of your plant. It may not need anything more than "plain vanilla" fertilizing (see the following.) On the other hand, the soil may lack trace minerals, may be too acidic, or may be too alkaline for your plant to thrive. You want to know that at the outset so that you can do something about it.

Soil testing can be done through your local Cooperative Extension Office or private laboratories. Listings can be found online or in printed directories. You can also buy your own kit and have some fun on your own while you save a little money.

Remember to take into account the mineral content of your water too. Test that as well to ensure it won't amplify or negate the effects of the fertilizer.

SELECT THE RIGHT FERTILIZER FOR YOUR PLANTS' NEEDS

You can fertilize your plant with a chemical or organic product, but my preference is always to use an organic product. It has a slower, gentler effect on a plant and improves soil structure, soil tilth, and soil health in addition to providing the plants with nutrients.

If you go the chemical route, choose a timed-release product to avoid a "jolt" or "burn" to your plant.

Assuming your fertilizer needs are not specialized, a product that's formulated for trees and shrubs will do the job for hydrangeas. Do not get caught using one that is balanced with equal amounts of each nutrient. That is a myth that needs to be broken. Using a balanced fertilizer actually overfeeds your plants. No plant uses NPK in equal amounts so you shouldn't apply it that way. Further, we know that phosphorus and potassium move very slowly in the soil compared to nitrogen, which moves quickly. What that means is that constantly adding phosphorous negatively affects your soil, and it runs off and pollutes waterways and water supplies—while not even achieving the desired effect. You will find that in some geographic locations you won't be able to buy phosphorous-laden fertilizers because of water pollution issues.

Research studies have found that flowering plants respond best to a fertilizer ratio of 3-1-2 or something close to that. The math wizards can recalculate that to 6-2-4 or 9-3-6. You get the picture. A "plain vanilla" version of this kind of fertilizer or one that is formulated for flowering shrubs works well (as long as it does not contain equal amounts of NPK as previously discussed). Don't worry, however, that your plants won't have the right nutrients to grow and thrive. In most cases, your native soil has just about what it needs to do the job with maybe a small amount of tweaking.

Organic formulations typically have lower numbers than chemical ones. When you fertilize organically, remember that what you apply to your plants is not always taken up (absorbed) by them. When they do take it up, it is slowly on their own schedule as they need the nutrients, not all at once as occurs with chemical fertilizers. This nutrient uptake is affected by pH, soil composition, and other soil factors. That's why soil testing is so important. It gives you the baseline you need to get up and running so you know exactly how to approach any nutrient deficiencies.

CORRECTLY TIME THE APPLICATION

An annual application is your minimal target, usually when the plant is dormant or about when it is starting to leaf out. You could make another application when it is flowering since that's when it's using most of its energy.

All fertilizing, like pruning, should stop after August 1 as you don't want to stimulate any new growth on the plant. At that point, you want the plant to start preparing for dormancy. Even if your plant is a rebloomer or you live in warmer zones and it's still putting out flowers after August 1, don't fertilize it.

APPLY CORRECTLY

The amount of fertilizer you use will depend on the size of your plant. There will be information on the package to guide you. More is not better! If the manufacturer wanted you to use more, they would tell you so they could sell you more.

If you use too much chemical fertilizer, you run the risk of damaging your plant to the point of killing it—not the desired result. You can always add more fertilizer, but you can't take it back after it's been applied. For this reason, I do not recommend those fertilizer spikes for trees and shrubs. They concentrate the material in one place and have a tendency to burn the roots of plants.

If your fertilizer is granular, make sure you scratch it into the surrounding soil surface area as directed on the package to prevent it from washing away during rain or irrigation.

CONSIDER COMPOST

One last reminder: It all starts with the soil. Hydrangeas like well-drained, humusy, fertile soil rich in organic matter. From season to season, this breaks down and so needs to be replenished regularly. Although not technically "fertilizer," the incorporation of compost improves drainage and adds important microbes on a gradual and steady basis while it improves soil health. Compost should always be part of your fertilizing regimen for these plants. A base of organic compost is a great amendment that will feed the plant slowly and evenly before you even get a chance to apply that balanced fertilizer.

WHAT FERTILIZER WON'T DO

If your flowers aren't the "right" color, fertilizer isn't the answer. Go back to the chapter on *Hydrangea macrophylla* on page 7 to learn how to change the color of your flowers.

If your plant isn't blooming, adding more fertilizer won't help. It's either the weather or cultural conditions causing the problem. Go back to the discussion about your specific hydrangea species to better understand why your hydrangea might not be blooming (page 25).

If you think your plant is sick, you need to find out what the problem is. Chemical fertilizer will add more stress

One brand of organic compost available at retail stores

as the plant tries to grow in response to the stimulus from fertilizer. It will not be able to use the energy it has to repair itself if it's trying to grow in response to the stimulus of fertilizer. On the other hand, compost will always help a sick plant; it's more like a tonic than a fertilizer.

Fertilizing by Hydrangea Type

Hydrangea macrophylla and H. serrata

Hydrangea macrophylla and *H. serrata* will perform better if you tweak the general fertilizer guidelines. You should aim to apply a good-quality, slow-release fertilizer once in spring or early summer as your plant breaks dormancy and begins to leaf out. If your plant is a rebloomer, a second application of fertilizer will boost that second flush of flowers. Apply that after that first bloom cycle as those new flowerbuds form.

When you buy fertilizer, pay attention to the middle number to ensure it isn't disproportionately high as too much phosphorous affects flower color. A chemical fertilizer with an NPK ratio of 12-4-8 can work fine for in-ground flowering plants. Keep in mind that too much nitrogen will lead to lots of green leaves and not many flowers so keep that first number under control. Or you can use organic rose food, which produces excellent results.

One brand of organic rose food available at retail stores

Containerized plants usually need more fertilizer during the growing season. Frequent watering leaches nutrients more quickly from the container medium than in regular garden soil so be prepared with some additional liquid applications to keep them thriving. How often you do this will depend on your situation, including factors such as the size of your container, climate, rainfall, how often you water your plant, and so forth. Sadly, there's no one-size-fits-all formula.

Hydrangea macrophylla and *H. serrata* can develop yellow leaves, which may lead you to believe they have iron chlorosis. But don't be so sure; it could also be a sign of nitrogen deficiency. If you're growing a pink-flowering, pH-sensitive plant, iron chlorosis is likely since iron becomes less available as pH increases. The yellow color indicating an iron deficiency will show up on newer leaves. On the other hand, if older leaves have yellowed, you're looking at a nitrogen deficiency, which needs correcting. To be sure, don't take any action before getting a soil test to determine pH and nutrient levels.

One brand of liquid organic fertilizer available at retail stores

Iron becomes more insoluble and less available to plants as soil pH goes above 6.5 to 6.7 (too alkaline) and will likely show up on pink-flowering *H. macrophylla* and *H. serrata*. High amounts of other elements such as calcium, zinc, manganese, phosphorus, or copper in the soil can make iron unavailable to the plant. A shortage of potassium in the plant or the soil will also reduce iron availability.

Additionally, insufficient iron in the soil may be the cause, but you won't know without a soil test. If the soil test indicates a need, you can lower the pH of the soil by adding sulfur, which will free up the iron, or you can apply the appropriate nutrients, and the iron deficiency will disappear. Applying nutrients will take longer as the iron has to be taken up through the vascular system of the plant. A lower soil pH means less iron gets locked up in the minerals. Rather than adding iron, freeing up the existing iron will get better results.

However, if your plant is adjacent to a lawn that you regularly lime, it's possible that it's getting the runoff from that annual lawn application. Dial down the lime application or be prepared to continually treat the hydrangea for chlorosis. (This problem can affect hydrangeas growing near buildings with cement foundations or concrete that leaches lime.) You can treat the problem with a foliar application of water-soluble or chelated nutrients (those that have been treated to enhance their availability to plants). This will temporarily correct the problem. However, it only helps the leaves that are on the plant during application. Several treatments per growing season may be necessary to keep the foliage green.

Chlorosis is a common problem so you may as well buy an inexpensive bottle of liquid iron and keep it on hand as you probably have the condition elsewhere in your garden. Using the liquid iron will give you a much quicker result. Apply the product as directed to easily solve this problem. You'll look like a genius!

Hydrangeas love to grow leaves and will do so at the expense of flowers so be careful not to overfeed them. The same thing will happen when they are overwatered. It's a delicate balance.

Last, be aware of unintended consequences. Hydrangeas sited

One brand of liquid iron available at retail stores

within the confines of a well-fertilized lawn or a septic system may also enjoy excessive nitrogen. The foliage will be fabulous, the flowers, not so much.

Hydrangea quercifolia

Like most woodland plants, *Hydrangea quercifolia* likes a slightly acidic soil so use your soil test kit to check the pH and aim for a pH between 5.5 to 6.5.

Since this plant has already set the current year's flowers by the time you fertilize it, you're fertilizing for general health. A properly formulated granular fertilizer would work well when applied in the spring as the plant is waking up. On the other hand, if you were to use a rose fertilizer you could be helping your plant by giving it the nutrients needed for next year's flowers. Only do this if your soil test showed a nutrient deficiency. I must admit that the only amendments I have ever made to the soil beneath my *Hydrangea quercifolias* over the course of the many years I have grown them are compost and shredded leaves.

Because of its woodland preferences, this hydrangea is especially fond of well-drained, humusy, fertile soil rich in organic matter. Apply all yearly in the spring.

Hydrangea petiolaris

Your climbing hydrangea is extremely versatile. It can tolerate acidic and alkaline soil (pH 5.0 to 8.0) so you shouldn't need to fuss with amending the soil for that purpose. In the twenty-plus years I have been growing this old-wood bloomer in many locations, I have never fertilized it. If your soil is thin or weak, however, then go ahead and add organic matter such as compost, shredded leaves, pine bark, and the like.

Remember, this is a vine that grows well in shade, which naturally comes from woodland environments. So try to mimic that environment at the planting site and you'll need to give the plant fewer inputs.

Hydrangea arborescens

All the general rules about fertilizing hydrangeas apply to *Hydrangea arborescens*, keeping in mind that this is a plant that grows in woodland shade and flowers on new wood. It can tolerate a wide pH range of 5.0 to 8.0 so it clearly is not fussy.

As with other hydrangeas, avoid high-nitrogen fertilizers. This is another hydrangea that naturally grows in forest soil characterized by well-drained, humusy, fertile soil that's rich in organic matter. This hydrangea also benefits from a yearly application of compost.

Scratch a general all-purpose shrub fertilizer into the top two to three inches of soil during the late spring. Rose fertilizers are excellent for this purpose.

On the other hand, if you were to do nothing, that would work too.

Hydrangea paniculata

All the general rules about fertilizing hydrangeas apply to *Hydrangea paniculata*. Because this hydrangea flowers on new wood, spring fertilizing and maintaining good soil health through a yearly application of compost will bring on the best flower production. This hydrangea can tolerate a wide pH range of 5.0 to 8.0.

Avoid high-nitrogen fertilizers and proximity to lawn runoff of nitrogen.

A general, all-purpose flowering shrub fertilizer scratched into the top two to three inches of soil in the late spring would be fine for this plant. It also responds well to rose fertilizer. However, it isn't fussy and doesn't require yearly fertilizing.

Hydrangea serrata 'Preziosa' showing its
beautiful late season colors

CHAPTER THREE

WATERING YOUR HYDRANGEAS: FIND THE RIGHT BALANCE

General Hydrangea Watering Guidelines

In an ideal world, if we all had automatic watering systems, I would tell you to set the system at one inch of water per week for all your hydrangeas. That system would also have a governor that would turn it off when there was sufficient rainfall so your plants wouldn't suffer from wet feet. Better still, we would get a nice, slow, weekly rainfall of about one inch during the growing season that would come at about three a.m. and allow foliage to dry before nightfall. Sadly, our world isn't ideal.

Assuming your plants are established, they should still be watered regularly. You can do the "knuckle test" to see how dry the soil is if the foliage doesn't already tell you. Push your index finger into the soil at the base of the plant, about 3 inches out from the center. If it's dry to the first knuckle, water the plant slowly until that soil is saturated at that depth. Go back in an hour and do the same thing to ensure your plant is sufficiently hydrated. If it's not, repeat.

Remember that all of the hydrangeas we've covered like *moist*, well-drained soil, moist being the key word here. That's your objective. You can miss a week or two but if your growing season turns out

A soaker hose laid at the drip line of *Hydrangea paniculata*. (Note the mulched base of the shrub.)

to be dry, your plant will show its displeasure in the form of parched leaves, fewer flowers that don't last, and weak colors. You get the picture. Soaker hoses and "quick connect" set-ups are inexpensive and enormously helpful tools for regularly watering thirsty plants.

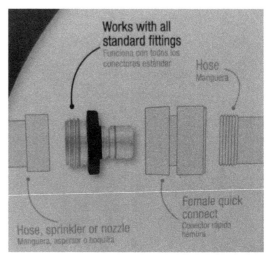

"Quick connect" parts for hoses sold in retail stores

Water all hydrangeas deeply at ground level and infrequently in order to draw its roots down into the deeper richer and well-fertilized soil that holds moisture. Do not water from overhead as that promotes fungal disease. If the only irrigation option you have is some kind of overhead set up, then do it in the earliest part of the

Installed quick connectors before connecting or mulching   Installed quick connectors after connecting but before mulching

day so the foliage has time to dry thoroughly. You don't want to contribute to conditions that foster fungal development and growth. With proper irrigation, your hydrangea will show its love in the form of more flowers for longer periods, lush and healthy foliage, disease resistance, better color, and so forth. In short, that's exactly what you want.

These two species get special attention because they are the troublemakers. (Because the other hydrangea species covered in this book are less likely to dry out as quickly, you are less likely to overreact and drown them.) The large leaves of *Hydrangea macrophylla* and *Hydrangea serrata* are the first to show signs of water stress when the sun starts to cook them on a warm day. They lose moisture through the many stomata (pores) on the leaves.

It's common for both of these hydrangeas to wilt and droop when they have been in the sun for several hours. To relieve the pain we feel at this sight, many gardeners rush out to flood the plants in an attempt revive them. Yes, the plants will perk up as they take up the moisture, but in the long run, when we do this, we invariably do more harm than good.

Remember, hydrangeas love to make leaves and if we provide excess water, the plants will do so at the expense of flowers. Secondly, the excess moisture will often suffocate the roots of the plants (by crowding out space for oxygen in the soil), leading to a slow and premature death. You can even give these hydrangeas too much water when they are watered using an irrigation system, so be watchful of that possibility.

Hydrangea macrophylla wilting in afternoon sun

What's a gardener to do when you see those droopy leaves and wilting flowers? Hard as it is, walk away and wait a few hours until after the sun has moved off the plants to see if they rehydrate on their own. You may even have to wait until the following morning. Do some weeding in another part of the garden, harvest some vegetables, or sit in the shade and catch up on your email. Only after you have evidence that those droopy leaves have not perked up should water be applied.

Based on the origin of its name (*Hydra* is Greek for water), many people think *Hydrangea macrophyllas* and *Hydrangea serratas* need more water than they actually do.

The best watering advice I can give you is to be observant. Notice what's going on in your garden on a regular basis so that you can immediately assess if your plants look out of sorts and need intervention. Use a rain gauge to help you keep track of how much water you're actually getting in your little corner of the world.

You have to learn to be a bit of a Sherlock Holmes and consider the interaction of weather, soil, mulch, and where your plant is sited to learn how best to water it to find the right balance of irrigation, neglect, and when to step in to take appropriate action.

A butterfly nectaring on *Hydrangea paniculata* Little Quick Fire®

CHAPTER FOUR

TRANSPLANTING: WHEN AND HOW YOU SHOULD MOVE YOUR PLANTS

The general rule for transplanting anything is to do it in the season opposite of the one in which it performs, i.e., its "off season." So if something blooms in the fall, transplant and divide it in the spring, essentially when it is dormant. For something that blooms in the spring, you would plan on moving it in the fall. So it is with hydrangeas. It depends on when they flower.

With hydrangeas, as with other plants, you have a choice whether to transplant early in the growing season (spring) or the fall. Keep in mind that early-season transplants will be much more dependent on you, the gardener, to provide sufficient water for the entire summer. If you don't have an automatic watering system, that can get old very fast as the season marches on, especially if it is a dry one.

Here are some other general guidelines.

PREPARE THE NEW SITE

Once you have chosen the best site you can based on your plant's needs (allowing for sunlight, soil, drainage, and moisture conditions), dig the receiving hole first to be sure you can accommodate the rootball. I can't tell you how many times I have hit "foundation" rocks (read GINORMOUS) that have thwarted my planting plans!

If you're okay on the receiving end, fill the hole with water and let it drain to be sure your drainage is adequate.

Receiving hole being tested for drainage

If it empties in less than an hour, your hydrangea will either die of thirst or you will be exhausted trying to keep it hydrated. This is an indication that your soil isn't water-retentive and first needs to be amended to hold moisture or that you need to pick a different site. If it takes a few hours to empty, you should be okay to plant into this hole. If it takes a day or more to empty, your soil is much too heavy in that spot and you need to seriously amend it or find a better site. You might want to do a pH test while you wait to ensure you have the right conditions for your plant and get a line on the types of amendments you may have to add to bring that space up to standards.

Transplanting is traumatic for a plant so I always recommend using some sort of mycorrhizae additive in the fill soil to help reduce transplant shock and establish roots. There are many choices on the market. Simply follow the label directions to help your hydrangea make this transition. The only other amendments to add at transplant time are compost or composted manure and whatever you have decided to apply to adjust the pH, if necessary.

PREPARE THE PLANT THAT YOU'RE MOVING

Water the plant the night before moving it to ensure that it is well hydrated. Depending on the size of your plant, a wheelbarrow may be necessary in addition to some burlap and a tarp. A garden buddy for an extra pair of hands and a strong back will also come in handy.

Hydrangea wrapped with bungee cord before being dug out

If your plant is large and you want to keep it that size, you may want to wrap it loosely with a bungee cord or somehow tie it to keep it together. Some plants can open up and splay once they have been dug completely around their base at the drip line.

DIG IT UP!

Carefully use your transplant spade to gently dig around the edges of your plant at the drip line without actually digging it up. Then go deeper and start to coax the plant out of the ground, trying to keep as much of the rootball intact as possible.

Slide the burlap underneath the plant and tie it around the rootball to keep it together. Now is when the plant might split, so you want to slide it onto that tarp and avoid actually lifting it. Here's where that garden buddy can really help you as you either drag the plant over to the new hole or lift it into the wheelbarrow for transport.

Hydrangea dug and placed onto a tarp for transport to new hole

MAKE THE MOVE

By now your newly dug planting hole should be ready to accept its new tenant. The water drainage has been tested, the proper amendments have been added based on your soil test, and your plant is good to go.

Now "puddle the plant in." Puddling in is a bit of a throwback to your childhood mud-playing days, except now it's a useful

Receiving hole ready for transplant

planting technique. Put your plant into the very wet hole that has just finished draining—it might even have some water still in the bottom of it—with some of the backfill soil. Then water the plant and the backfill slightly to get a good muddy mix going. Tamp it slightly to remove the air pockets. Let that set for a bit, then repeat that process until the plant is completely in the ground and there is bit of water sitting at its crown and slowly percolating down to the roots, essentially creating a puddle. This process not only waters the plant well, but also eliminates air pockets during and after backfilling. Make sure the plant doesn't sit deeper in its new hole than it was before you moved it. The only exception to this is if the plant had been heaved out of its previous spot for some reason such as burrowing creatures or freezing temperatures.

Amendments should be thoroughly integrated into the backsoil and the planting hole along with the native soil. No peat moss, Holly-tone, Miracid, or anything else should be added at this time. Create a firm soil collar about 2 inches high and about 4 inches out from the base of the plant to capture the water and allow it to be slowly absorbed by the soil. Or, better yet, lay a soaker hose a few inches away from the base of the plant so you can just turn it on to ensure your transplant gets off to a good start.

The last part of the transplant process is to mulch your newly transplanted hydrangea. You want to put down a 2- to 4-inch layer of mulch like stones, wood chips, shredded leaves, cedar mulch, or other mulch depending on the kind of hydrangea you have moved and where you have moved it. The chapter on mulching on page 85 gives specifics on what type of mulch is best for each kind of hydrangea. This will keep the soil moist and protect the roots. It also helps to keep the soil temperature even as your plant goes into dormancy and experiences seasonal ups and downs.

CARING FOR YOUR TRANSPLANT

Keep a close watch on your plant after you move it to be sure it gets enough water as it heads into dormancy. If you move it in the fall, especially after it has lost its leaves, you won't be able to detect water stress as those new roots develop. Watch the weather, do some knuckle tests, use your rain gauge, and be ready to provide supplemental irrigation if there is a shortfall of natural precipitation.

During the following two summers your transplant may need a little more attention while those fragile roots are still getting established. A soaker hose at the plant's base will help a great deal as long as you don't overdo it. Be prepared to spritz the foliage if the plant wilts even if the soil at its base is moist to the touch.

Transplanting Instructions by Hydrangea Type

TRANSPLANTING *HYDRANGEA MACROPHYLLA* AND *H. SERRATA*

When: The best time to transplant *Hydrangea macrophylla* and *H. serrata* is in the fall after they have finished flowering and are about to go dormant. You want to give them enough time to grow roots and get established before the ground freezes; they need a good six weeks to do that. Depending on where you live, you could be transplanting as early as September 1 or as late as November 15. You need to do the math and work that out. Figure out when your ground freezes. Then count back 6 weeks. That's the last date you should be transplanting your hydrangea. It's that simple. If you live where the ground doesn't freeze, you need to transplant no later than February 1 so the plants establish themselves in time to give you your full season of flowers. Think sooner rather than later.

Where: As discussed in the chapter on *Hydrangea macrophylla*, choose the best site you can based on your growing zone allowing for sunlight, soil, drainage, and moisture conditions. Don't forget the desired overhead protection of winter persistent foliage if you're in a cold zone. Morning sun is best.

Preparing the Site: The one difference from general transplanting guidelines regarding *Hydrangea macrophylla* and *H. serrata* is to make sure to do a pH test and apply appropriate soil amendments if you want to manipulate the flower color. If not, *que sera sera.*

TRANSPLANTING *HYDRANGEA QUERCIFOLIA*

Transplanting an oakleaf hydrangea is the same as transplanting a *Hydrangea macrophylla* in terms of timing; both plants need to finish flowering and are about to go dormant.

When: As with *Hydrangea macrophyllas* and *H. serratas*, plan to do this job in the fall. You want to give a plant enough time to grow roots and get established before the ground freezes; it needs a good six weeks to do that. Depending on where you live, you could be transplanting as early as September 1 or as late as November 15. You need to do the math and work that out. If you live where the ground doesn't freeze, you need to get that transplanting done no later than February 1 so the plant gets established in time to give you your full season of flowers. Think sooner rather than later.

TRANSPLANTING *HYDRANGEA PETIOLARIS*

The job of moving your climbing hydrangea will be a little different than your other hydrangeas. The roots of this plant are fibrous and spreading and so your preparation will be more demanding. In my experience, I have found it easier simply to buy a new plant but you may relish the challenge. Let me lay it out for you.

When: In terms of timing, you want to do this when the plant is dormant. This vine flowers on old wood and if the flowers are important to you and you don't want the irrigation chore for the summer to get the transplant going, then wait until late summer or fall to tackle transplanting *Hydrangea petiolaris*.

Like other fall transplants (about which you may have already read), you want to give it enough time to grow roots and get established before the ground freezes; it needs a good six weeks to do that. Depending on where you live, you could be transplanting as early as September 1 or as late as November 15. You need to do the math and work that out. If you live where the ground doesn't freeze, you need to get that transplanting done no later than February 1 so the plant gets established in time to give you your full season of flowers. Think sooner rather than later.

Preparing & Digging the Plant: A day or two before you plan to make the move, prune the plant back to about one to two feet in length. You can leave some side shoots on it, but you want the plant to make a successful transition so you don't want it to have too much top growth to support. Water what's left of the plant by puddling the area at its base.

When you dig the roots of this plant, you'll find they are spreading and fibrous. Those multiple root systems may require you dig several holes to extricate this plant. Be ready!

Carefully use your transplant spade to gently dig around the edges of the plant and start to coax it out of the ground, trying to keep as much of the rootball intact as possible. Slide burlap underneath it and tie it around the roots to keep them together. Slide everything onto the tarp and either drag the plant over to the new hole or lift it into a wheelbarrow for transport.

Preparing the site for _Hydrangea petiolaris_: When you dig the receiving hole, remember to also install a very strong trellis or arbor. _Hydrangea petiolaris_ is a vigorous grower. Follow the general planting instructions for preparing the site (page 75) but make sure to install a trellis.

TRANSPLANTING _HYDRANGEA ARBORESCENS_

Hydrangea arborescens is an early-summer new-wood bloomer. Following the ground rule of moving plants the season opposite of the one in which they perform, the best time to move this plant is late summer/fall.

Plan to do this job after your _Hydrangea arborescens_ has finished flowering and is about to go dormant. Like other fall transplants, you want to give it enough time to grow roots and get established before the ground freezes; it needs a good six weeks to do that. Depending on where you live, you could be transplanting as early as September 1 or as late as November 15. You need to do the math and work that out.

At the risk of being repetitive (though I believe that just reinforces the concept), if you live in the warmer parts of the country where the ground doesn't freeze, you could tackle this job in late winter, getting that transplanting done no later than February 1. The objective is to give the plant enough time to get its roots established before it starts to put on the growth for the new season, growth that will bear those glorious flowers we all love.

TRANSPLANTING *HYDRANGEA PANICULATA*

Hydrangea paniculata is another new-wood bloomer, but this one performs in midsummer and beyond. Following the ground rule of moving plants the season opposite of the one in which they perform, you have a choice here of moving the plant in early spring or late fall, during both times the plant is either fully dormant or approaching dormancy.

If you move it in late spring when it is technically dormant, you are demanding that it work on root establishment when you really want it to work on new stems and flowers for the upcoming season. Too many agendas, if you ask me. Further, by moving it at the start of the summer, you put irrigation demands on you, the gardener, for the entire season that otherwise wouldn't be there. Not exactly my cup of tea. Given a choice, I vote for a later season transplant plan, which means you'll be doing it in the fall after your *Hydrangea paniculata* has finished flowering and is about to go dormant.

It's worth repeating that if you live in the warmer parts of the country where the ground doesn't freeze, you could tackle this job in late winter. The objective is to give the plant enough time to get its roots established before it starts to push growth for the new season, growth which will bear the current season's flowers. In this scenario, you again make the plant much more dependent on you, the gardener, to provide sufficient water for the entire summer season. That can get old very fast.

The transplanting process is the same as for all hydrangeas; there's no magic formula here, just some hard work.

A border of *Hydrangea arborescens* Invincibelle Mini
Mauvette ™ is a show stopper!

PART TWO: GIVING HYDRANGEAS THE BEST CARE

CHAPTER FIVE

MULCHING: MORE THAN MOISTURE CONSERVATION

Always mulch your hydrangea for the same reasons you mulch anything else: keep weed growth/competition down, conserve moisture, regulate soil temperature, prevent soil erosion and compaction, reduce lawn mower damage, and improve garden appearance.

General Mulching Guidelines for All Hydrangeas

Check the mulch around hydrangeas in the spring after the soil has warmed up and reapply if necessary. Applying it too early will keep the cold in, which is not what you want to do. You might need to reapply in the fall before colder temperatures settle in your area to protect the roots and retain moisture through its dormant season.

Place irrigation/soaker hoses underneath the mulch to prevent moisture loss. When you refresh the mulch at the beginning of the season, you might as well take the time to inspect and correct your hose set-up if necessary.

Spread mulch about 3 to 5 inches deep from the stems of the plant out to the drip line. Remember to keep the mulch at least 2 inches from the base of the plant so rodents don't nibble on the bark of your plant or decide to live in the shelter of its spread. You might have to crawl under the plant to inspect for this clearance each season,

A soaker hose laid at the drip line of *Hydrangea paniculata* in mulch before being covered

probably twice a year; mysterious things happen to move that mulch around and you don't want to find your plant has been munched by hungry mice, voles, squirrels, and the like while you were warming your toes by the fire. The other reason to keep the mulch away from the stems/trunk of your plant is to prevent wetness; you don't want the mulch, which keeps the soil damp, to also keep the stems/trunk wet. That will only weaken them and make then susceptible to insects and disease.

MULCHING GUIDELINES BY HYDRANGEA TYPE

The various species of hydrangeas can and should be mulched slightly differently for maximum plant health.

Hydrangea macrophylla and H. serrata

For pink-flowering hydrangeas, use neutral mulches like stone chips over a base of compost as those stones can add lime to the soil when plants are watered.

For blue-flowering beauties, use organic matter such as shredded leaves, peat moss, and bark chips because those materials will continue to acidify the soil and improve the organic matter profile of your soil as they break down.

If you use this same organic matter on pink-flowering plants, you will counteract whatever you are doing to produce pink flowers so be aware of the potential impact of those organic mulches.

Hydrangea quercifolia, Hydrangea arborescens, and Hydrangea petiolaris

All three of these hydrangeas grow best in shade and/or woodland environments with slightly acidic soils. They prosper when they're mulched with bark chips, cedar, shredded leaves, and compost. All of those materials will add nutrients to the soil as they break down while also providing the typical benefits of mulch.

Hydrangea paniculata

As a full sun lover, your *Hydrangea paniculata* responds more favorably to mulch than any of the other hydrangeas we've covered. Yes, it is drought-tolerant once established, but it will do far better without the stress of dry conditions. The flowers will be more prolific and will last longer with better color and the plant will thrive versus just grow. Mulch is one easy way to achieve that, so why not?

Hydrangea arborescens 'Annabelle'

PART THREE: TROUBLESHOOTING HYDRANGEA PROBLEMS

ALTHOUGH GENERALLY TROUBLE-FREE, HYDRANGEAS DO HAVE THEIR SHARE OF CHALLENGES IN THE GARDEN, INCLUDING DEALING WITH PESTS AND DISEASES. HERE ARE THE MOST COMMON HYDRANGEA PROBLEMS AND HOW TO SOLVE THEM.

The elegant variegated foliage of *Hydrangea macrophylla* Light-O-Day® brightens any garden

CHAPTER SIX

HYDRANGEA DISEASES: WHAT THEY ARE AND WHAT TO DO

Hydrangeas are subject to several diseases, most of which are fungal in nature. Although generally not fatal, they are disfiguring and mar the appearance of the plant.

FUNGAL DISEASES

Fungal spores initially come into the garden on the wind, but once there you can't ignore them. Plants can be infected early in the season but may not show the disease until later on as heat, humidity, summer rain, and irrigation all create the cultural conditions for the disease to manifest itself and proliferate.

Cercospora Leaf Spot

Cercospora is one of the more common fungal leaf spot diseases and will usually show up towards the end of the summer. It can show up on *Hydrangea macrophylla*, *H. arborescens*, *H. paniculata*, and *H. quercifolia*.

The spots are irregular and develop a tan or gray center surrounded by a purple or brown border. Entire leaves may turn a yellowish green as the fungus continues to produce spores, which then further infect the plant and others in the garden. The plant will show the leaf spots first at the bottom of the plant. Additional spotting will occur higher

A leaf from *Hydrangea macrophylla* showing *Cercospora* leaf spot

in the plant foliage as spores are splashed or moved into upper leaves from irrigation, rain, or a gardener working in the landscape.

Diseased leaves (fallen or attached to the plant) are the primary sources of spores so it stands to reason that garden sanitation is a key measure of control for this condition. Take action as soon as you notice the spots on the leaves and be vigilant up to and at the close of the gardening season. (Remove diseased leaves from the plant and rake up and discard diseased leave that have fallen to the ground.) If you have had problems with *Cercospora* for more than one season, it's likely that the spores are hanging out in the mulch, just waiting for the right conditions to re-inoculate your plants. Removal and replacement of said mulch is an advisable strategy to get a handle on *Cercospora*.

Botrytis

Botrytis also likes to attack hydrangeas, especially *H. macrophylla* leaves, flowers, buds, and blossoms. It needs a run of several consecutive days of cloudy, humid, rainy weather to develop. You will see small water-soaked spots that expand into reddish brown irregular blotches. The flower petals fade to brown and become covered by the gray growth of the fungus, thus, the common name "gray mold." It spreads quickly and turns all in its wake to mush, leaving infected flowerbuds to drop off and foliage to wither and die but not before spreading more spores.

Like most fungal diseases, *Botrytis* spores initially come in on the wind and then survive in plant debris. They are easily dispersed by wind and water so control is critical. Popular plants like geraniums are carriers of the same pathogen so remove old blooms quickly, especially if the geraniums are close to hydrangeas since the most common source of *Botrytis* spores is dying plant material.

Diseased leaf from *Hydrangea petiolaris*

Anthracnose

Anthracnose is the third fungal disease you might see on hydrangeas. This one likes *Hydrangea macrophylla* and goes for both the leaves and the flowers. Like the others, it likes hot, wet weather.

Anthracnose on a hydrangea leaf

However, the leaf spots for *Anthracnose* look very different than the others we've been discussing. These spots are a bit larger than those of other diseases. These spots are also sunken and rounder than others and look a bit like bull's eyes with concentric rings. Spots also appear both on the foliage and flowers at the same time throughout the plant.

Diseased plants are the main source of *Anthracnose* but, like other fungal diseases, if it is in the garden it probably originally came in on the wind.

Powdery Mildew

Powdery mildew is perhaps the easiest disease for the average home gardener to recognize since we see it so frequently on other garden plants such as monarda, phlox, squash, cucumbers, and so forth. It looks the same when it shows up on *Hydrangea macrophylla, H. serrata, H. arborescens,* and *H. paniculata.* The white, cottony powdery mildew fungus spreads remarkably quickly and can disfigure a plant practically overnight, in addition to stunting it. Unlike most of the fungal diseases that

Hydrangea macrophylla showing powdery mildew on leaf surface affect hydrangeas, this one does not spread when the weather is wet. It actually prefers dry conditions. So that dry summer that parches your plants is also ideal for this disease to spread. Powdery mildew fungi are serious threats in warm and dry conditions as long as the relative humidity is high.

Rust

Rust is another easily recognizable disease on hydrangeas as it exists on other ornamentals in the garden, such as hollyhocks. *Hydrangea arborescens* is the one you need to monitor for this disease; it sneaks in on the undersides of foliage with its telltale small orange spots, usually near the end of the growing season. If you're not certain the disease is there, lightly rub the leaves with a gloved hand over a plastic bag to see if you get an orange dust—those are the spores of the fungus that you have now caught in that plastic bag.

Cut off all infected leaves and discard in a garbage bag to stop the disease from spreading. Then thoroughly clean the glove to prevent yourself from spreading the spores to any other plant.

If you miss removing any infected leaves, they will turn brown, wither, and die, ensuring those spores will winter over and reinfect the plant next season. Plus, those spores will spread on the wind (which is probably how you got them) and through overhead irrigation.

TREATING FUNGAL DISEASES

In most cases, the fungal diseases for hydrangeas will make a plant look ugly but make no mistake, successive seasons of attack will weaken plants, resulting in fewer flowers, pale colors, and stunted growth—everything you *don't* want. The fixes are relatively easy.

First, make sure you avoid all overhead watering and do your irrigating early in the day so foliage has a chance to dry.

The second important fix is to allow good air circulation between and through plants—don't crowd these babies! You might even need to thin out some plants by doing some judicious pruning if a plant is overgrown in its center.

Next, be relentless about garden sanitation—clean up and remove all hydrangea leaves. That's easier said than done, at least in my garden where hydrangeas are about the last plants to lose their leaves. By then it's cold, and sometimes those leaves freeze to the ground, making them difficult to rake up, and I usually need to plant my garlic or get my holiday shopping done.

If you have had any leaf spot issues, it may be time to replace the mulch to ensure there are no active spores hanging around.

Try not to work among your hydrangeas in wet conditions. That's a good way to spread fungal diseases and their spores. Wait until foliage is dry to deadhead, mulch, and do any general grooming.

If you're not already a convert, a good habit to get into is to regularly disinfect any tools you use on your plants so as not to unwittingly spread disease. A quick spray of Lysol® on pruners, cutting, and digging tools does the trick. If you prefer not to use an aerosol, use isopropyl alcohol (70 percent strength) from your medicine cabinet in a spray bottle to spritz your tools. It's impossible to get into the nooks and crannies of pruners any other way. Alcohol surface wipes work well to do the same job on larger surfaces. Stay away from bleach solutions as they are corrosive to tools, plus you then have extra steps of rinsing off the bleach and thoroughly drying the tool to prevent rust.

There are excellent commercially available organic fungicides you can use to treat fungal disease without poisoning yourself or the planet. Look for products formulated with active ingredients including hydrogen peroxide, Neem oil, *Bacillus subtilis*, or potassium bicarbonate. Make sure they are registered to treat the disease you have for the plant in question. That information will be stated on the label, as will the instructions on how to use the fungicide along with any precautions. I do not recommend using copper-based products because they have residual effects on soil and soilborne organisms.

In terms of when to spray, prevention is the operative word. If you had the disease last season, scout for it early and spray immediately. That means you should purchase your fungicide and have it ready to spray *before* you see anything.

You can, of course, let it go. That's a personal decision only you can answer depending on your tolerance for ugliness.

ROOT ROTS

Root rots are the other category of diseases to which hydrangeas are susceptible. Here's where planting in a site with good drainage and providing proper irrigation become critically important to plant health, as the fungi that cause root rots proliferate in wet conditions.

There are several root rots. All come from soilborne fungi that exist in practically all soils. They are activated when your plant gets too much water. The fungus grows and attacks the roots of the plant. The result is plant death.

The list of root rots affecting hydrangeas includes *Phytophthora* root rot, *Pythium* root rot (also called water mold), and mushroom root rot (also called *Armillaria* root rot), which is most commonly found on oakleaf hydrangeas.

Sometimes, after noticing a plant wilting, if you grub around at its base that may lead to the discovery of a white fungus under the soil or black fungus beneath the bark of some stems.

Or, in the case of mushroom root rot, you may see dozens of the disease's telltale caramel-colored mushrooms sprouting at the end of the season after heavy rains. In most cases, you will need the help of experts from your local Extension Service to diagnose the existence of root rots including the specific one your plant might have.

TREATING ROOT ROTS

Sadly, while there is no cure for root rots, it helps to stop watering the plant. Depending on your energy level and interest, you could dig it up and cut away the diseased roots, then thoroughly disinfect your gloves, and cutting and digging tools.

If it's in a container and you want to keep it, remove the plant from the container and check the drainage. Replace the container and potting medium if you see some disease-free roots. Cut away the diseased roots and dispose of them along with the diseased container mix. Sterilize the container if you plan to reuse it (whether with the repotted plant or any other plant). Disinfect any tools you use as well as your gloves.

For your in-ground plant, even if you don't dig it up but you decide to keep it in the hopes it recovers, make sure you cut away any diseased stems, shoots, and so forth.

Anytime you work on a diseased plant, always disinfect any tools you use as well as your gloves.

BACTERIAL DISEASES

Several bacterial diseases attack hydrangeas, and they are often mistaken for fungal leaf spot diseases. They have much in common in that they winter over in plant debris, and are spread by splashing water or by working with the plants when they are wet. As with fungal disease control, disinfecting pruners, avoiding overhead irrigation and wet foliage, strict garden cleanup, and providing adequate plant spacing for good air circulation are all strategies to prevent the spread of bacterial diseases. Often, bacterial leaf spot is brought in on new plants from nurseries where they were watered with overhead irrigation. Once the plants are in your garden and not watered every day from above, the problem may clear up over time.

Unfortunately, bactericides have limited effectiveness treating these diseases. Removal might be your only option, which, if you look on the bright side, can be an opportunity to get a better, newer plant. Just be sure your site is perfectly cleaned up and disinfected or you will be back where you started.

A leaf from *Hydrangea quercifolia* showing bacterial leaf spot

A word of advice...the photos in this chapter are provided to enlighten you and make you aware of what to look for on your plants. I strongly encourage you to use them as your compass to provide direction so you can determine when something is wrong. Once you have done that, a live consultation with local horticultural experts is the next step to get an accurate diagnosis since many fungal and bacterial issues can be misdiagnosed based only on photographs. Local Cooperative Extension offices and Agricultural Experiment Stations are available throughout the country to assist home gardeners with plant diagnostics. Only after getting their advice would it be prudent to confirm your application of a fungicide or take other action to remedy your situation.

The hard-to-find but garden-worthy lacecap
Hydrangea macrophylla 'Frau Reiko'

CHAPTER SEVEN

HYDRANGEA INSECTS: WHAT THEY ARE AND WHAT TO DO

Before we get into the discussion of insects and your hydrangeas, I must pause to give you my strong position on gardening organically, specifically as it relates to the use of pesticides and insecticides.

I encourage you to manage your garden and hydrangeas in accordance with basic principles of Integrated Pest Management (IPM). For our purposes, IPM is defined as an approach of managing pests that considers prevention, avoidance, monitoring, and suppression. When all else fails and you need to intervene by using a pesticide, use one of a biological nature that maximizes safety and reduces risk to the gardener and the environment.

To start with, be aware that only 2 to 3 percent of all insects can actually harm plants. The other 97 percent just fly and crawl around as nature intended and are part of an ecological system that needs them to exist to keep everything in balance.

With that in mind, I offer my rules of the road as you consider how to treat for insects.

1. First rule of IPM is **DO NO HARM**, i.e., protect beneficials—the good guys in the garden—including ladybeetles, worms, frogs, spiders, and so forth.

2. Always know the enemy (life cycle of the insect, how its develops and progresses) before doing anything so you know when to apply treatment for the most effective response.

3. Remember that you need to have some bad bugs for the good bugs to eat. If the bad bugs aren't around, the good bugs fly away. Complete annihilation is not the objective in integrated pest management.

4. The first rule translates into a basic philosophy to start with the treatment that has the lowest impact.

5. You need to be an observant scout and look for changes in your plants. Inspect the undersides of foliage and note if there are unusual flying insects and so forth. You want to catch budding problems and address them ASAP.

If you decide to treat, this is the prescribed order:

- Use a strong stream of water to wash off insects without damaging your plants, where feasible.

- Try hand-picking: Although time-consuming this inexpensive technique addresses small insect populations, such as Japanese beetles. Check the undersides of leaves, and squish bugs you find or possibly remove the leaf entirely. Taking a few minutes to do this regularly is a very effective control strategy to prevent serious problems.

- Use sticky traps: Traps attract insects with color and/or odor, holding them on a highly sticky surface. These work well when the insects first appear, especially for insects that produce multiple generations in a season and for pest control if you don't know what's ailing your plant. (At the very least, you can catch a few to identify them.)

- Use insecticidal soap or horticultural oil: Spraying these compounds suffocates insects such as whiteflies and aphids. Beneficials aren't affected but you will need to reapply after rain. Sprays need to be applied primarily on leaf undersides where these insects hide—handy because the sun can cause burn spots on sprayed leaves.

- Neem oil at 70 percent kills insects at all stages of development: egg, larvae, and adult with no effects on beneficials. The active ingredient, azadirachtin, works as an antifeedant, hormone disruptor, and by smothering. It forces the insect to stop eating and prevents the bug from transforming into its next stage of development by disrupting regulatory hormones. Its one drawback is that it's effective only in cool, overcast, damp conditions.

- Grow plants near your hydrangeas that will draw beneficials into your garden. These plantings are known as insectaries; they will attract good bugs, which will then consume the bad bugs. That will cut down dramatically on your need for any intervention, which will save time, money, and energy and reduce your anxiety about this whole subject. See the Resources section on page 159 for websites that specialize in this.

INSECTS THAT AFFECT HYDRANGEAS

Although hydrangeas are generally carefree, there are some insects that will find their way onto your plants. Most are harmless and will cause only minor cosmetic damage so you don't need to get too anxious about them.

Leaf Rollers or Leaf Tiers

The first insects you might notice will arrive on *Hydrangea arborescens*. They are commonly called leaf rollers or leaf tiers. It's a moth that forms a web between two leaves to create a cocoon-like structure to rear its young (caterpillars), which will grow up to become more moths. Pretty familiar lifecycle, right?

You can remove the affected foliage, which will otherwise die if you let the natural cycle continue. Or you can squish the leaves, again resulting in the foliage dying. You can also unfurl the leaves, gently drown the young caterpillars in some soapy water, and let the foliage

Two leaves of *Hydrangea arborescens* webbed closed by leaf rollers

Leaves of *Hydrangea arborescens* opened to expose and destroy leaf roller larvae

live. The leaves will be a little bruised but they will make it just fine. That's my preferred approach unless, of course, you have too many of them and it becomes an onerous task. Or you can just leave them alone; nothing bad will happen except you'll lose a few leaves. This moth will produce another generation before the season ends.

Sucking, Piercing Insects

Then there are a group of sucking, piercing insects that live to literally suck the life from your plant as they feed on the sap to enrich their own lives. These include aphids, scale, and whiteflies. They all look different but the result of their activity is the same: leaf curl and premature death of foliage. Before you see them, you might notice ants all over your plant that have been drawn to the insects' sticky, sweet excretions called honeydew. Or you might see "sooty mold," the blackish fungal growth that grows on honeydew.

Aphids

These pests flock to new green plant growth but as a plant matures and the foliage gets tougher, they will be less likely to hang around. A strong stream of water will dislodge aphids. As the ants feed on the honeydew they also protect these pests from their natural enemies. You could coat the stems of the plant with Tanglefoot® pest barrier, which is similar to the sticky substance on the yellow sticky traps. The Tanglefoot® will keep the ants away. You could also scrape aphids into a bowl of soapy water if they are congregating in a few places. Diatomaceous earth is another product you can use. Apply it to the ground where the aphids crawl to destroy the aphids' outer layer. If your own insectary hasn't produced enough hungry beneficials, place an order for lacewings or ladybeetles (especially their larvae) or find a local source for them. They are voracious when it comes to aphids. If you must spray, insecticidal soap or Neem oil will do the trick.

Whiteflies

While these insects have a four-stage development cycle, you won't see a thing until the adults emerge in a cloud. Then you'll want to panic, but don't. You need to know that they have several generations a season (about once every 25 to 30 days) so it's wise to get a handle on them right away. Aside from the fact that they look different from aphids and have a different lifecycle, they have the same honeydew, sooty mold, and so forth. So what you would do for aphids, you would also do for whiteflies, right down to treatments, with the exception of the diatomaceous earth as the whiteflies don't crawl…they fly.

Oyster Shell Scale

This pest on hydrangea is a little more complicated to deal with. These insects usually infest the upper stems of your plant. You get your best shot at noticing them before the plant leafs out. That's when you should scout for them. At this point, the insect itself (the crawler) is "sleeping" under the hard shell of the scale and won't emerge until the weather warms in late spring or summer. By the time you see sooty mold or ants harvesting the honeydew, treatment will be much more difficult. When it comes to scale, you want to catch these crawlers either upon emergence or before they come out. That way you literally stop them in their tracks before they get away. This is one time when natural enemies and beneficials can really help you. If you scouted when the plant was dormant, you should have enough time to get those beneficials lined up. Parasitic wasps and certain lady beetles are especially effective should you decide to go that route. Worst case, you use organic sprays after the crawlers are out, such as insecticidal soap, horticultural oil, or Neem oil. If you miss the timing when the crawlers are around, your treatment options diminish greatly.

Spider Mites

If you have ever grown a houseplant, you should be familiar with spider mites. They are hard to avoid since they like the hot, dry conditions of a winter-heated home. You'll notice either the webbing between the leaves where the actual insect lives or yellow dots (called stippling) on the leaves. Using a hand lens or magnifying glass to inspect the foliage, you should be able to actually see these tiny insects and their eggs. A dry summer allows them to proliferate so a quick spray of water early in the day on a regular basis wouldn't be a bad idea since spider mites also like a dusty environment. Their damage is mostly cosmetic, causing deformities. Spider mites are one of the harder insects to control but if you have predators like lady beetles around and use your hose, you shouldn't have to take stronger measures.

Four-Lined Plant Bug

Four-lined plant bug damage is very distinct. Once you see it, you will always be able to identify the round, brown, sunken spots it leaves on foliage. It can sometimes be mistaken for disease; however, the spots are so uniform that you will soon be able to tell the difference. The insect spends the winter as an egg mass in linear slits near the branch tips of woody plants. Those eggs hatch after the plant has broken dormancy, allowing the nymphs to feed on the new foliage. A month later, the adults emerge to feed, mate, and lay eggs for the following season.

Sprays are rarely needed to treat four-lined bugs. *Hydrangea paniculata* and *H. arborescens* shouldn't have a problem with these, since you'll be pruning them back to some degree and essentially removing those potentially problematic branch tips. However, *Hydrangea macrophylla* could incur damage. It would behoove you to scout for the egg-laying sites when your hydrangeas are dormant in late autumn or spring before the foliage emerges so that you can selectively prune or cut out the egg masses. You can use insecticidal soap or horticultural oil on the nymphs before they molt into adults. It's nearly impossible to spray once the adult form has emerged: they are fast and cleverly drop to the ground to hide under debris. Lest you forget, they have wings and fly away if disturbed.

Japanese Beetles

I am sorry to tell you that Japanese beetles do indeed like hydrangeas, especially *Hydrangea quercifolia*. Rather than wring your hands and lose sleep over that, here are my recommendations for dealing with this pest.

Remember: one of our rules is to know the lifecycle of the beast and when it is susceptible to what. You'll be glad to know that your tax dollars are hard at work on this since Japanese beetles are a major agricultural issue for this country. There are scores of people who continually work on managing this insect because of the insects' effects on farmers and crops across the country. Our friends in the USDA have provided us with a fantastic graphic on the lifecycle of the beetle so we know when it is most advantageous to do what. Herewith, the Japanese beetle lifecycle:

| JAN | FEB | MAR | APRIL | MAY | JUNE | JULY | AUG | SEPT | OCT | NOV | DEC |

Of course, depending on the weather and your geographic location, the timing of treatment here is fluid. In warmer years, the grubs will emerge earlier and the adults will start feeding on your plants sooner. In cooler springs, the adults will come out later. Where I live, I can pretty well expect to see my first beetles around July 1. At that point, even though they are hungry, they don't start feeding immediately. They are more concerned first about sending out an aggregating hormone to call their friends to the party. Then, like bears just out of hibernation, they voraciously begin feeding. You should be one step ahead of them and start your removal program *before* they send out that signal or minimally in conjunction with it.

Plan on a two-pronged attack. Part one is to go after the adults in the current season. Part two will be to go after the larvae, which will take up residence after the feeding is over. That's where you can make the most headway for the future.

For part one, here's how you can manage your Japanese beetle population:

Hand-Picking: This is very effective, especially in the early morning when cooler temps make them lethargic. Done early enough in the season, it can reduce egg laying, further reducing the population of grubs later on.

Neem Oil: Neem, as you already have learned, is a valuable organic pesticide. It's biodegradable and breaks down in the soil without harming the environment. Keep in mind you need to spray during cool, damp, overcast conditions so pay attention to the weather.

Trap Plants: Japanese beetles are attracted to certain plants. You can use the plants as traps to make hand-picking them easier. Some of these plants have the added benefit of being poisonous to the Japanese beetle. Just be aware that what is poisonous to the Japanese beetle can be harmful to people and animals as well. Good trap plants are four o'clocks (poisonous), larkspur (poisonous), castor bean (poisonous), borage, marigolds, light-colored zinnias, and white roses.

Veggie Pharm: This product has been reported to kill Japanese Beetles on contact. Follow label directions. Do not spray in sunlight or during hot temperatures. It at least stuns them so you can hand-pick.

For part two, you now focus on going after the grubs that like to live in your lawn. They feed on those grass roots before they emerge as adults to feed on your ornamentals:

Bacillus thuringiensis galleriae: This is a natural soil- and foliage-dwelling microbe effective against both the adult and grub forms of Japanese beetles, Oriental beetles, Asiatic garden beetles, European chafer, Northern masked chafer, Southern masked chafer, and May and June beetles. It's available in granular and liquid forms and presents no risk to lady beetles, pollinators such as butterflies and bees, parasitoid wasps, aquatic animals, birds, or domestic pets.

Beneficial Nematodes: These are microscopic parasitic worms, many of which benefit our environment. *Heterorhabditis bacteriophora* is parasitic to Japanese beetle grubs but harmless to other plants, insects, and animals. Soil moisture is essential for this nematode to take effect and attack grubs. Water before and after you apply nematodes to your lawn. Directions always come when you order them. **TIMING OF APPLICATION IS CRITICAL.**

Milky Spore Disease: *Bacillus popilliae* is a naturally occurring disease of Japanese beetle grubs that is not harmful to humans or other creatures. Several commercial dusts are available. Grubs eat grass roots that have been dusted with the spores, become infected with the disease, die, decompose, and then release more spores into the soil. This is not usually a quick fix as it can take up to two seasons to significantly reduce populations. However, it can provide years of protection once it's established. **TIMING OF APPLICATION IS CRITICAL.** It's much more successful in warmer climates than in zone 6.

Hydrangea quercifolia Gatsby Moon® shows its incredibly dense flower head

CHAPTER EIGHT

VARMINTS: PROTECTING YOUR HYDRANGEAS FROM WILDLIFE

The sad truth is that all hydrangeas are tasty to rabbits and deer so even if yours have not yet been nibbled, that doesn't mean it won't happen. Plant toxicity has little or no effect on varmints.

Deer nibbling

Young, unprotected *Hydrangea arborescens* showing deer damage

The rabbits are most destructive to small plants as the foliage can be at their low level. Once your plants get taller than the animals' height, they generally outgrow the "rabbit danger zone." Of course, the newer varieties that stay small will forever be targets for rabbits.

Strategies to protect your hydrangea plants both from deer and rabbits are no different than those you would use to protect any other plant, including fencing, repellent sprays, systemic repellent products, free-roaming dogs who will chase them from your garden, granular fertilizers that are known to be unpleasant to deer, and so forth.

Hungry roaming rabbit

I have had great success using the deer sprays (all of which are nontoxic). In winter, some gardeners use what I call "snow pots" to keep both deer and rabbits off the plants. This is simply an inverted nursery pot held down with a rock, but it only works for small plants.

Overturned nursery pot protects a small hydrangea from wildlife in winter

Your local Cooperative Extension office can guide you, as this is truly a regional issue with which they will have local expertise. Local garden center experts can also help you in how to handle this problem.

If your plant is one that flowers on new wood, you can adopt a *laissez-faire* attitude during the winter when maintenance is a little harder in the North and let the deer "help" you prune. But then you must get things back under control when the temperatures warm up and start your protection program so the munching stops. The plants will need to be tidied so they can set their flowers for their seasonal show and the wildlife will have to be disabused of the notion that your garden is their dinner table. Sometimes that is easier said than done.

A group planting of
Hydrangea serrata Tuff Stuff™

PART FOUR: HYDRANGEAS IN THE LANDSCAPE

GET MORE OUT OF YOUR HYDRANGEAS. HERE'S HOW TO INTEGRATE THEM INTO YOUR HOME LANDSCAPE AND GARDEN, NO MATTER WHERE YOU LIVE.

A hydrangea in a container adds a decorative
touch to any pathway or entrance

CHAPTER NINE

PROPAGATION: MAKING MORE HYDRANGEAS

Before we get into how to propagate your hydrangeas, we need to get clear on the legalities of doing this. If the plants you want to propagate have a trademark (™) and are patented, if the label has PPAF (Plant Patent Applied For) or a plant patent number, or maybe you read somewhere on the plant tag or label "propagation strictly prohibited" or "asexual propagation prohibited," then by making more plants you're breaking the law. You might think that restriction applies to people other than home gardeners but you would be wrong. Legally, you can be fined for propagating patented plants. The reality is, however, that plant patent infringements on the part of amateur gardeners are not pursued by patent owners unless those infringements are profit-making. Making more patented plants seems to be one of those things that most home gardeners do without blinking, despite the fact that it's illegal.

Make sure the plants you propagate for others are "in the public domain." You can easily check that by doing an internet search. Use the specific query "unpatented hydrangeas" to identify which ones you can legally propagate without running afoul of the law.

For the purposes of this chapter, the following guidance applies to working with plants that are unpatented and without trademark.

WHEN TO PROPAGATE

A softwood cutting, also called a semi-ripe cutting, is one that is new and green. These cuttings are taken in early summer, and they're your best shot for success. The ideal cutting will break between your thumb and forefinger. If the shoot just bends, it is too soft and will rot before it roots. If it won't bend at all, it's too woody and won't develop roots for this purpose.

Always try to take your cuttings and do your propagation early enough in the growing season so your new plants can get into the ground before the season closes down. It usually takes about 4 to 6 weeks for hydrangeas to grow roots. Unless you have a greenhouse, be mindful that babying newly propagated plants through the winter indoors is risky, with low success rates.

PROPAGATION TECHNIQUES

There are four distinct ways to multiply your hydrangeas.

Division

This is the practice of dividing a shrub you already have that has multiple stems coming from its base. It will not work with the lollipop form of hydrangea, as that has a single trunk, which is not divisible. Using a sharp spade, take a piece of the shrub away from the "mother plant" and place it in another part of the garden. You would use the same technique described in the previous section on transplanting, on page 75, in terms of digging out the selected section and preparing the receiving hole.

Rooting Cuttings in Water

This propagation method is also pretty easy and one that you might have done by accident somewhere in your past: root a cutting in water. You might want to ensure your plant is well hydrated either by watering it the day before and/or taking your cutting early in the day before the plant experiences any moisture loss. Using disinfected pruners, take a stem cutting from the plant that does not have flowers or buds on it. Remove all the foliage except the top leaf, and cut the stem down to about 5 inches, making the cut about one-quarter inch above that bottom leaf node of your cutting. The leaf node is where the plant has growth hormones and where it will produce growth and, therefore, roots. Removing the leaves along the cutting means the plant can use all its energy to make roots. Place the cutting in a clean, clear vase or glass filled with water. Be prepared to change the water often to prevent bacteria buildup. A clear vessel will let you see the roots as they form.

Once the plant has a fistfull of roots, it's time to plant it into a sterilized potting medium so that it can start growing. Keep it in a container for several weeks so it gathers strength before planting it out into the garden.

Rooting into a Container

To root cuttings directly into a container you need to have the absolutely strictest sanitary conditions for all of your tools and potting materials. Bacteria and mold can infect things in a heartbeat and destroy all your hard work. You also might want to gather some useful materials: a Sharpie, maybe a popsicle stick or two to place in your container to tag your cuttings, potting soil, disinfected containers, clear plastic bags, clean empty beverage bottles, and rooting hormone.

Materials for propagation

Using those same disinfected pruners, take a stem cutting that has not had any flowers or buds this season. Try for one about 5 or 6 inches long. If you can't find one that size, cut a longer one down to size from the top. Mark the top of that stem with a Sharpie so you know which end is up because once you cut those leaves, it might be hard to figure that out. Remove the bottom two leaves and cut the remaining leaves on the stem in half.

Fill the sterilized pot, which will house the cutting with the proper container mix, make a receiving hole for the stem with a dibber or a pen/pencil, and water the mix to settle it. Add more mix if necessary and make sure you don't lose your opening for the stem in the watering process. Have some rooting hormone handy and sprinkle some into the top of the container or another small cup to use as a dip; you don't want to contaminate the entire jar of rooting hormone in case there is some bacteria lurking on your cutting.

A common rooting hormone available at retail stores

Dip the bottom of the stem, including the now bare leaf nodes, into some water to make the rooting hormone adhere, then dip the stem into the rooting hormone. Place the rooting hormone-covered stem and -leaf nodes into the open hole in the container and gently firm the soil up around it, being careful not to disturb the rooting hormone. The roots will be stimulated to grow from those leaf nodes so it's important that they be covered in the rooting hormone and the moist potting medium. Water the pot gently and well, letting it drain. You want the soil to be moist, not waterlogged.

Be careful not to bury the stem too deeply: you want to be sure there is enough oxygen in that container for the roots to form. Add a couple of wooden skewers or bamboo rods that are taller than your cutting on either side of it. Now cover your pot with plastic using those skewers/bamboo to keep the plastic off the leaves of your stem. This essentially creates a mini-greenhouse. You could also do this with an empty clear plastic beverage bottle.

Hydrangea macrophylla stem cutting

A beverage bottle used to convert a pot to a mini-greenhouse

Plastic bag used instead of a bottle to make a mini-greenhouse

Keep the cutting in a bright, shady spot until roots form, which should take about two to three weeks. Don't water until and unless the top of the soil feels slightly dry; you risk rotting your cutting. You could test it along the way by giving it a gentle pull. If it resists, you'll know that it's the roots at work.

Layering

I view layering as the lazy gardener's successful propagation technique. It's such a joyful surprise when you tug on what you think is an errant branch of a shrub only to find out it is actually a rooted extension of a "mother plant."

I think it's the coolest way to make more plants and often happens by accident with so many shrubs. It's my absolute favorite technique since you need to do so little.

All that's required is a low branch on your plant that makes contact with the soil. If you can't manage that, you can always get

Hydrangea arborescens shoot discovered with roots at its base

that branch to touch soil in a container that rests on the ground at the base of the plant.

A low branch was held down with a rock to allow new roots to form. A new plant is ready for transplanting.

Keeping the branch attached to the "mother plant," make sure it's predominantly shaded and wound the lower part of the branch where it makes contact with the soil (or the dirt in the container). Place a large rock or a brick on the top side of that branch to ensure the soil contact remains constant, cover it with more soil, water it, and keep it moist. Stake the branch that will eventually become your new plant; then let nature takes its course.

Check it every now and then to guard against that branch drying out. To ensure success, some gardeners dust rooting hormone on the wound before settling the branch into the ground or the container. In a few weeks, roots will form at that wound, and you will be able to cut the rooted stem away from the mother plant to grow it on either in the container or in a new planting hole. What could be easier?

One reason hydrangeas are so reasonably priced is that they propagate so easily. About the only special item you need is rooting hormone, and a little bit of that goes a long way. Oh, and of course some patience.

Just imagine how satisfying it will be when you can gaze at a garden full of plants that you have propagated yourself, not to mention the money you will have saved along the way. There's no reason why you can't be successful making more of these beautiful garden-worthy plants using any of these propagation techniques.

Hydrangea paniculata Tickled Pink® is a lovely
addition for smaller spaces

CHAPTER TEN

HYDRANGEA TOXICITY: BEAUTY AND THE DEADLY BEAST

I'm always a little awestruck when I learn that something beautiful is deadly. And so it was when I first found out about hydrangea toxicity. But then I had the same feeling about the nightshade family of vegetables: tomatoes, eggplants, peppers.

All parts of hydrangeas are toxic; they contain a cyanide-like compound known as glycoside amygdalin, which is poisonous. It is concentrated in the flowers and buds and can also be found in the leaves. Poisoning can only happen, however, if a very large quantity of leaves, buds, and/or flowers are ingested. The result is severe gastroenteritis. Large mammals and humans can suffer significant discomfort if they ingest enough, but there are no known cases of death from it.

If you wanted to mimic some reported European thieves, you could dry hydrangea flowers and/or leaves, roll them with tobacco into cigarettes, and smoke them for a cheap high. It seems that dried hydrangea flowers mimic the effects of tetrahydrocannabinol (THC), the active ingredient found in *Cannabis* (marijuana) plants. Leaves are also used this way.

The bottom line is that hydrangeas are poisonous but being poisoned by them is very unlikely. However, it stands to reason that the smaller the mammal, the more vigilant you need to be as it would take a lot less for those smaller bodies to be negatively affected by the poisons in this plant. Ergo, keep a close eye on small pets and children in the garden.

Sadly, this toxicity isn't enough to prevent wildlife like deer and rabbits from feeding on these plants. See Chapter Eight, on wildlife, for more information.

Hydrangea macrophylla 'Color Fantasy' winter protected by *Hydrangea paniculata* and conifers in a zone 5 garden

CHAPTER ELEVEN

HYDRANGEA HARDINESS: A TRICKY BUSINESS

The 2012 USDA Plant Hardiness Zone Map is the standard by which gardeners and growers can determine which plants are most likely to thrive at a given U.S. location. The map is based on the average annual minimum winter temperature, divided into 10-degree F zones.

But—and this is a big "but"—it is not an absolute. You should consider it a guide since we all have microclimates in our growing zone.

For example, when I enter my zip code into the interactive USDA map at http://planthardiness.ars.usda.gov/phzmweb/interactivemap.aspx, that database comes back to tell me that I am in growing zone 6. However, I can tell you with certainty that many zone 6 plants perform as annuals in my garden. The exception to that is where my property faces south. There, and only there, do I have zone 6 growing conditions and, in some cases, zone 7.

Why is that? For one, I live on a hill and that elevation change affects temperature. My property is also in a cold pocket, which has another effect. Last, in the areas where I have damp soil, those gardens hold the cold longer because of the moisture. That soil moisture causes a later spring thaw and earlier fall chill, all factors affecting my growing zone.

That means my zone 6 hardy plant better be ready to take zone 5 temperatures or be prepared to become compost.

So what does this means for hydrangeas? Hardiness becomes a fine point of distinction when it comes to *Hydrangea macrophylla*. Yes, there are cultivars rated hardy to zones 4, 5, and 6, and yes, you can expect those plants to survive at those zone-specific temperatures but it is the roots that will surely survive at those zone-specific temperatures. Stem hardiness, on the other hand, in this case the flowerbuds, may not enjoy the same level of hardiness. That's why, after a "bad winter," you'll get a nice green bush but no flowers. The roots were hardy as promised, but the stems that produce the flowers were not. Sad, but true. Sometimes *Hydrangea serrata* gets caught in this web but not always. As has been discussed, it has better cold tolerance.

Be heartened: those roots will produce new stems and your *Hydrangea macrophylla* plant will live to see another day. But old-wood plants might not have flowers. The new-wood cultivars, however, will give you flowers if you treat them right. Just as soon as that new stem can get its mojo working, it may not have the typical early season flush, but certainly will flower before the summer ends.

The other two old-wood bloomers, *Hydrangea quercifolia* and *Hydrangea petiolaris*, have better stem hardiness and cold tolerance and, like *Hydrangea serrata*, usually pull through when *Hydrangea macrophylla* doesn't.

The low hardiness ratings and new-wood bloom habit of *Hydrangea arborescens* and *Hydrangea paniculata* preclude any winter dieback issues. You'll be giving them an annual spring haircut for tidying, shaping, and rejuvenation while you take the opportunity at the same time to freely cut away any winterkill without affecting your current season's bloom.

USDA PLANT HARDINESS ZONE MAP

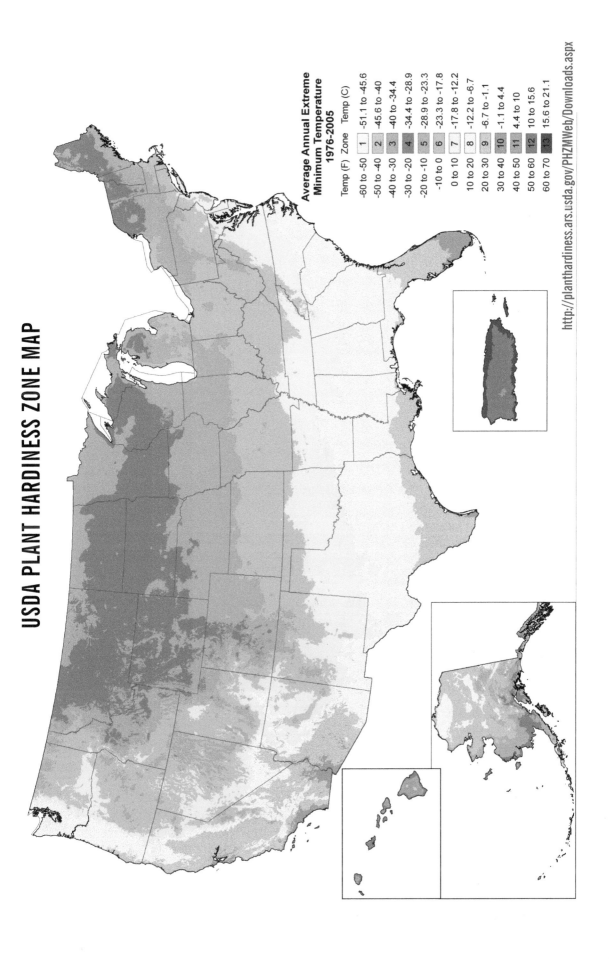

Average Annual Extreme Minimum Temperature 1976-2005

Temp (F)	Zone	Temp (C)
-60 to -50	1	-51.1 to -45.6
-50 to -40	2	-45.6 to -40
-40 to -30	3	-40 to -34.4
-30 to -20	4	-34.4 to -28.9
-20 to -10	5	-28.9 to -23.3
-10 to 0	6	-23.3 to -17.8
0 to 10	7	-17.8 to -12.2
10 to 20	8	-12.2 to -6.7
20 to 30	9	-6.7 to -1.1
30 to 40	10	-1.1 to 4.4
40 to 50	11	4.4 to 10
50 to 60	12	10 to 15.6
60 to 70	13	15.6 to 21.1

http://planthardiness.ars.usda.gov/PHZMWeb/Downloads.aspx

Hydrangea macrophylla Everlasting™ Magical Amethyst is a kaleidoscope of color

CHAPTER TWELVE

HYDRANGEAS FOR WARM STATES

It's worth noting that special care needs to taken growing hydrangeas in the warmer parts of the country. For example, if you garden in Texas, Arizona, and the other warm states like Georgia, for example, your growing conditions are much different than in the cooler parts of the country. If you're reading this, you already know that simply means you need to make some adjustments to the general cultural ground rules that apply to other growing zones.

The USDA hardiness zone map is an excellent starting point. It helps gardeners better understand how plants will respond both to cold and warm temperatures. If you're in a zone warmer than 6, that heat tolerance rating for hydrangeas becomes more important. In the high zones of 8 or 9 some hydrangeas won't make it.

When you grow hydrangeas in warmer zones, you must be sure the soil can remain moist without becoming waterlogged. High levels of organic matter that hold moisture will work their magic while also providing drainage. A covering of 2 to 4 inches of mulch around all hydrangeas in these areas is critical to seal in life saving moisture. This will keep the roots damp without setting up conditions for root rot.

Your biggest challenge will be the sun, so siting your hydrangea where it gets late afternoon protection is critical. Morning sun is best, as has already been mentioned. South- and west-facing exposure will spell certain death as blazing sun will fry the plant, unless you can site it in the protection of large, dense shade trees (be careful to avoid root competition). You could even get away with northern exposure if the light is bright enough. Full shade, however, won't work if you want flowers. Even with these sitings, the daily climb of seasonal ambient temperatures will parch the plant so you still need to monitor moisture levels on a regular basis and irrigate as needed. That irrigation should always be slow and deep, so that the plant can take the water up into its system and the roots won't get waterlogged. Make sure the plant has a soil "collar," a solid ring of dirt about 3 inches high that encircles the base of the plant. That way when you water it, you can create a puddle, which can slowly drain, preventing the water from running off.

If you want to grow hydrangeas in desert climates you will be challenged. Hot, dry, exposed sites won't do. The lack of humidity will consistently parch the foliage no matter the steps you take in terms of soil preparation, amendments, or irrigation. The one hydrangea which might make it, however, is *Hydrangea quercifolia*. Again, after amending the soil properly and allowing for irrigation needs, the oakleaf hydrangea will survive if planted on those less sunny east- and north-facing sites.

Warm zone gardeners must also pay attention to the same weather vagaries we all have like unusual cold temperatures or early spring bud blasts. For the most part, those occurrences are few and far between.

On the other hand, I envy anyone who grows hydrangeas in zone 6 or warmer; you have dozens more options for spectacular *Hydrangea macrophyllas* for which I lust.

Gardeners in zones warmer than 6 also have some extra time to do those late-season chores such as transplanting. The rest of us have to get that job done in late summer/fall to ensure we get plants settled and root formation underway before the ground freezes.

A big advantage for growing *Hydrangea macrophylla* in zone 6 or warmer is repeat bloomers. Many of us can only dream of having these flowers for more than a few short months. Properly managed, repeat bloomers can provide flower color for an extended season with very little "downtime." *That* gives me a bad case of zone envy.

One hydrangea that warmer zone gardeners may find truly unique and lovely for their gardens is *Hydrangea arborescens* ssp. *radiata*, also known as Silverleaf hydrangea. This one is commonly found in garden centers in the southeastern states and can be found as "Snowy hydrangea" as well, named so because of the silver undersides of its foliage. It's most noticeable, as you might imagine, under breezy conditions, which create a two-toned effect of a deep green top side against the white underside. The flower is also different in that it is more of a lacecap look than a mophead. There's also a double-flowered version of Silverleaf hydrangea for even more garden delight.

Last, in the warmer zones you have a better container option—no need to worry about frostproofing them. You can grow your hydrangeas very successfully this way and treat them as needed, be it weather, soil, fertilizing, and so on. It's a terrific way to grow *Hydrangea paniculata* standards, think sentries to a garden entrance or at the end of a garden path, drawing you into the garden or a focal point in the center of a garden. True, maybe you can't grow extremely large specimens this way, but this is another approach to consider if you simply must have this plant in your garden and have been stymied up to now.

Hydrangea paniculata Little Quick Fire® in a container

Hydrangea macrophylla in a mixed container

CHAPTER THIRTEEN

GARDEN USES FOR HYDRANGEAS

HYDRANGEA MACROPHYLLA

You can use *Hydrangea macrophylla* just about anywhere in any garden. Around the globe, there is no absence of photos of it in cottage gardens, in shrub borders, in woodland settings, and enhancing pool settings in the ground as well as in containers. Its preponderance in coastal gardens demonstrates its tolerance for salt spray and salty air. They are used as specimen plants, cut flowers, dried flowers, and in wreaths. *Hydrangea macrophyllas*, especially the lacecaps, are bee magnets and add a particular appeal to bee meadows. It's common to see them used as indoor plants as they are popular in the florist trade for forcing, especially around Easter and Mother's Day. Always keep the frost sensitivity of this plant in mind if you garden in a cold zone, as that can ruin your garden design in a season following uncontrollable weather situations.

Hydrangea macrophylla Endless Summer® used as pathway edging in woodland setting

Hydrangea macrophylla Midnight Duchess® can be used to great advantage in a mixed container

Hydrangea macrophylla Let's Dance Moonlight® used to line a walkway

GARDEN USES FOR *HYDRANGEA MACROPHYLLA*

The market for *Hydrangea macrophylla* continues to expand. Gardeners find this plant irresistible and have an insatiable appetite for it. For that they have been rewarded each season with improved choices.

Not only are there hardier introductions, but now there are *Hydrangea macrophyllas* in diminutive sizes that are well suited to containers or can be used

Hydrangea macrophyllas flank a stone wall

Hydrangea macrophyllas used as foundation plants

to replace perennials. Smaller sizes fit into today's smaller gardening spaces, plus a compact plant is easier to "winter protect." So if you do live in one of those colder climates, you have the option of bringing your plants in from the elements in a bad winter. Or you can easily insulate a few small plants with leaves, and even bubble wrap.

Your borders and containers will burst with color when you wander away from the traditional blues and pinks of old. The reds have arrived! I think the only colors in the spectrum that we don't have *yet* are yellows and oranges, and I would bet someone is working on that as I write this.

Add to all of that the fact that *Hydrangea macrophyllas* are fast growers with a long season of color and are almost trouble free. And with rebloomers, I'm hard pressed not to find room for just about any of them, especially at end of season sales.

Hydrangea serrata Tiny Tuff Stuff™ in a mixed container

Early flowers already pruned awaiting second flush

HYDRANGEA SERRATA

Like *Hydrangea macrophylla, Hydrangea serratas* are extremely versatile garden performers. The lacecap and mophead flowers in pinks, blues, and now red, look fabulous in any garden, be it a border, container, or woodland—you name it. The newer smaller *H. serrata* options work well in place of perennials as they are about the lowest maintenance plant I know: rarely bothered by insects, almost entirely

Hydrangea serratas in a shade garden with hostas

disease-free, and little or no deadheading needed in exchange for a long season of bloom and color. Some cultivars even have the capability of developing red coloration in their fall foliage as the temperatures cool. What's not to like?

Hydrangea serrata 'Bluebird' in garden setting

Hydrangea arborescens Lime Rickey® makes an attractive hedge

HYDRANGEA ARBORESCENS

Hydrangea arborescens makes a traffic-stopping hedge and an attractive mass planting. It can be placed in a woodland garden since it tolerates shade so well, as well as being used as a specimen plant. It's also great in containers! The large-sized 'Annabelle' has worked well to camouflage an air conditioning unit at my home for many years. Its ability to take shade makes it a natural as a background for a perennial border. And of course, if you're designing a native plant garden, this shrub's pollinating power puts it top on the list as *de rigueur*.

Hydrangea arborescens Invincibelle® Spirit in a part shade garden

Hydrangea arborescens White Dome® in a part-shade garden. Note typical bee activity for lacecap flowers.

Hydrangea 'Bounty' shows its lovely blue green foliage and strong stems

Hydrangea arborescens Incrediball® showing its sheer size

HYDRANGEA QUERCIFOLIA

Hydrangea quercifolia's preference for shade makes it right at home in a woodland setting with lots of light. You can use it in coastal gardens as it is salt tolerant. Shrub borders and specimen plants are just a few ways to showcase this beauty. When used as a mass planting to form a flowering hedge, it makes a much more attractive screen than a fence. As a cut flower, the large flowerheads look stunning in bouquets either as dried or fresh specimens or when woven into decorative wreaths.

Hydrangea quercifolia accented by a blue spruce in a mixed planting

Hydrangea quercifolia accented by a golden thread cypress in the foreground for color and texture and by a red-foliaged plu in the background for color in a mixed planting

Hydrangea quercifolia Gatsby Gal® lights up the side wall of a white building awaiting dramatic, deep fall color of its autumnal foliage

Hydrangea quercifolia Jetstream™ adds variety to the mixed plantings of a hydrangea garden

Hydrangea quercifolia accented by a red barberry in a mixed planting

HYDRANGEA PETIOLARIS

As a very low-maintenance shade lover, climbing hydrangeas are superb as privacy screens. They are favorites in shade gardens and as adornments for arbors and trellises. They cover rocks and stumps and can camouflage debris piles and other unsightly blights on

Hydrangea petiolaris vigorously covering a trellis

the landscape. This plant makes a dense groundcover and can blanket steep embankments to hold the soil. Although it is deciduous, its exfoliating bark adds winter interest to northern landscapes.

Add to all of that the fact that deer don't seem to like it much, and you have an extremely versatile vine with year-round interest that has more than earned its stripes as a garden-worthy plant.

Hydrangea petiolaris stems grown to cover a stump

Hydrangea petiolaris happily climbing a tree

HYDRANGEA PANICULATA

Hydrangea paniculatas work well in borders and as specimen plants. They're also useful in containers. They are colorful as full sun hedges as well as in other mass plantings. The large flowerheads look stunning as cut flowers in bouquets as dried or fresh specimens. Smaller cultivars fill gaps in borders in place of perennials, providing months of carefree summer color.

Hydrangea paniculata 'Baby Lace' in a mixed container

The selections are so varied these days, ranging from 18-inch-tall blooming machines to giants of 6 feet or more, that you would be hard pressed not to find room for one or more of them somewhere in your garden, considering they are nonstop flowering machines. They are fast growers, dependable performers, and garden worthy in all respects. With the right care, their summer parade of flowers is a continual source of pleasure.

Hydrangea paniculata Bobo® in a mixed planting

Hydrangea paniculata Fire Light® growing in a container

Hydrangea paniculata is the one you're most likely to see as a lollipop, sold as a "standard." The growth is on the top of the bare trunk where it balloons into stems and flowers. This is a plant you can place in a container and closely manage its size, soil, and fertilizer. You can move it around the garden when the light changes to be sure it gets the right conditions. This is not to say you can't plant it directly in the ground where it will also work in all the ways already discussed. However, *H. paniculatas* in lollipop form look especially handsome as sentries at garden entrances, at the end of a garden path drawing you into the garden, or as a focal point in the center of a garden. How cool is that?

Dried *Hydrangea paniculata* stems in a basket

Two Pee Gee hydrangea standards (lollipops)

Hydrangea Bobo® plays nicely with *Hydrangea macrophylla* and others in a mixed border

GLOSSARY

ACCENT PLANT: a plant that is used to catch your attention by its placement in the garden or by virtue of its contrast to its surroundings.

ACIDIC SOIL: soil with a pH lower than 7. Can be helpful if you want a blue *H. macrophylla*, which is pH sensitive.

ALKALINE SOIL: soil with a pH higher than 7. Can be helpful if you want a pink *H. macrophylla*, which is pH sensitive.

ANTHRACNOSE: a fungal disease causing leaf spots, leaf drop, and so on.

APICAL BUD: a flower bud at the tip of a stem.

APICAL DOMINANCE: the ability of the terminal bud to control the growth of flowers and branching side shoots on the length of an entire stem.

AGM: Award of Garden Merit bestowed by the Royal Horticultural Society of England to a plant based on several criteria amounting to outstanding garden performance.

AUXIN: a hormone that controls plant growth.

AXIL: the junction between a leaf and a stem.

BIOLOGICAL CONTROL: a means of dealing with pests and diseases that uses naturally occurring predators and parasites.

BONEMEAL: a naturally high phosphorous fertilizer made from crushed and powdered animal bones that works more slowly than a chemical phosphorous-based fertilizer; used to stimulate flowering and strengthen root growth.

BOTRYTIS: a disfiguring fungus, also known as gray mold, that attacks plants.

BUD: an undeveloped leaf, flower, or shoot.

BUD HARDINESS: the ability of a flower bud to produce taking into account harsh cold or icy conditions, a particular issue for *H. macrophylla* cultivars.

CHELATE: a chemical complex that contains iron, thereby making it readily available to plants to treat chlorosis.

CHLOROSIS: a deficient nutritional condition in a plant that can show up as yellowing foliage; it could be caused by an issue with nitrogen, iron, or magnesium.

CLIMATE ZONES: designated geographic growing areas incorporating different climatic conditions based on the average lowest annual temperatures.

CLIMBER: a plant that grows vertically using tendrils, adhesive rootlets, twining stems, and so on.

COMPOST: decomposed organic matter that is used as a fertilizer, topdressing, mulch, and so on.

CULTIVAR: a shortened name standing for "cultivated variety," which is a plant bred either by seed or vegetatively for specific characteristics.

CUTTING: a part of a plant removed for the purpose of propagation to create a new plant.

DEADHEADING: the removal of spent flowers.

EVERBLOOMING: a plant that produces new flowers nearly continually throughout the growing season.

FERTILE: the part of a flower having an embryo capable of developing into a new plant.

FERTILIZER: a material that supplies one or more of the major nutrients of Nitrogen, Phosphorous, and Potassium as well as micronutrients.

FLORET: individual small flowers of an inflorescence.

FLORIFEROUS: having an abundance of flowers.

FLOWER: the reproductive organ of most garden plants, sometimes producing seeds.

GENUS: botanical category denoting a group of species sharing similarities in flower form, and so on.

GRAY MOLD: see *Botrytis*.

GROWING ON: caring for a seedling or cutting until it is ready to be planted in the garden.

HORTENSIA: a name commonly used for big leaf hydrangeas.

INFLORESCENCE: a cluster of flowers arranged in a particular way.

LACECAP: flower form of *H. macrophylla* consisting of central fertile flowers ringed by outer, sterile ray flowers.

MICROCLIMATE: local conditions of elevation, wind, and so on that might affect plant growth at any given site.

MOPHEAD: flower form of *H. macrophylla*, which looks like a pom-pom.

MULCH: a protective layer of material spread over the base of plants to keep in moisture, inhibit weeds, and so on.

MYCORRHIZAE: microscopic organisms in soil that form relationships between roots and soil fungi to promote plant health.

NATIVE: a plant that grows naturally in a particular region and was not introduced from somewhere else.

NEW WOOD: stems that are grown in the current season.

NODE: slightly enlarged growth part of stem from which other stems, leaves, or flower buds emerge.

OLD WOOD: stems that were grown in prior seasons.

ORGANIC: term that describes any material that contains carbon and is derived from living or once-living plants or animals.

PANICLE: branched flower form consisting of several inflorescences, which bloom from the bottom up.

PETAL: the brightly colored leaves that surround the reproductive parts of a flower.

PETIOLE: the stalk of a leaf.

PH: the logarithmic measure that denotes acidity or alkalinity on a scale of 1 through 14, with 7 being neutral. Below 7 is acidic and above 7 is alkaline. On the pH scale, pH 10 is ten times more alkaline than pH 9 because it is a logarithmic scale, not an absolute one.

PRUNING: the act of cutting back and cutting out growth in plants for the purpose of spurring new growth as well as removal of dead, diseased, and damaged plant parts.

REMONTANT: a plant that sets buds which will mature and bloom in the same growing season. It reflowers sporadically or continuously from new seasonal growth. Sometimes called a repeat bloomer.

REPELLENT: a product used on or near plants to deter insects or animals from feeding on them.

ROOTING HORMONE: a natural or synthetic compound used to stimulate plant cuttings to produce roots to enhance vegetative propagation. Can be liquid or powder.

ROOT ROTS: a fungal disease that can infect plants grown in overly wet and poorly drained soil.

RUST: a fungal disease that appears on hydrangea foliage.

SEPAL: one of the series of the outermost part of a flower, arranged in a ring outside the petals. All the sepals make up the calyx.

SERRATED: usually refers to leaves, which are sawtoothed and forward-pointing.

SHOOT: an aboveground stem.

SIDEDRESS: to apply granular fertilizer to a plant alongside it to stimulate it.

SLOW-RELEASE FERTILIZER: a fertilizer that works slowly over time so as not to jolt the plant, e.g., compost or bonemeal.

SOAKER HOSE: a very porous hose with many small perforations which allows water to slowly seep or leak.

SOFTWOOD OR SEMI-RIPE CUTTING: a cutting taken from a young, soft stem of a plant for the purpose of propagating since it roots so readily.

SOIL AMENDMENT: any material incorporated into the soil to improve structure, fertility, aeration, and so forth.

SPECIES: group of individual plants within a genus that share many characteristics; the second part of a plant's botanical name.

STANDARD: a plant pruned to grow on a single stem with a bushy head of branches on top. *H. paniculata* is offered in this form.

STEM CUTTING: a cutting, excluding the tip, used for propagation that includes one or more nodes.

STERILE: a flower without the ability to reproduce; it will not produce seeds.

STOMA/STOMATA: microscopic pores on the undersides of leaves which allows a plant to breathe. This is also where hydrangeas lose their moisture when exposed to warm temperatures and hot sun.

SUCKER: an underground shoot that emerges from the parent plant and grows on to be a new plant. *H. arborescens* readily does this.

TERMINAL: borne at the tip of a shoot or stem. *H. paniculata* flowers emerge this way.

TIP CUTTING: a pruning cut made at the tip of a shoot to remove the apical bud. For reblooming hydrangeas, this removal can cause nascent flowers to begin their bloom cycle.

TRELLIS: a support structure erected for vining plants in the absence of buildings, and so on.

UMBEL: a flower cluster resembling an upside-down umbrella. All flower stalks come from the same point n the stem.

VEGETATIVE PROPAGATION: making more plants by duplicating the parent and not using seeds.

Hydrangea macrophylla Double Delights™
'Perfection' displays it spectacular flower form

REFERENCES

Baysal-Gurel, F., M. N. Kabir and A. Blalock, 2016. Root Diseases of Hydrangeas. Tennessee State University Publication ANR-PATH-4-2016.

Busman, L., Lamb, J., Randall, G., Rehm, G., Schmitt, M. 2002. "The nature of phosphorus in soils". Regents of the University of Minnesota. https://www.extension.umn.edu/agriculture/nutrient-management/phosphorus/the-nature-of-phosphorus/

Dirr, M. A. 2004. Hydrangeas for American gardens. Timber Press, Inc., Portland, OR.

Dirr, M. A. 2012. Hydrangeas: Breeding, selection, and marketing. Plant Introductions, Inc. Watkinsville, GA. http://www.plantintroductions.com/hydrangeasbreedingselectionandmarketing.html

Friday, T. 2012. Leaf spots may mean a fungal disease. University of Florida Newsletter, 07/14. https://bay.ifas.ufl.edu/newsletters/2012/07/14/leaf-spots-may-mean-a-fungal-disease/

Hagan, A. K. and J. M. Mullen. 2001. Diseases of hydrangea. Alabama Cooperative Extension System, Auburn University, Auburn, AL. ANR-1212, Oct., 2001. http://www.aces.edu/pubs/docs/A/ANR-1212/ANR-1212.pdf

Hawke, R. Low-maintenance, long-lasting hydrangeas. 2011. Fine Gardening. Oct 2011, 32-37. https://www.chicagobotanic.org/sites/default/files/pdf/plantinfo/hydrangeafinegardening2011.pdf

"Impacts of Lawn Fertilizer on Water Quality" University of Vermont. Compiled by Sara Davies, Matthew Reed, and Sarah O'Brien February 22, 2001, http://www.uvm.edu/~vlrs/doc/lawnfert.htm

Lancaster, N. and Wesley, W. 2008. The RHS Trial of *Hydrangea paniculata*. RHS Plant Trials Bulletin, Number 23 December 2008. https://www.rhs.org.uk/Plants/PDFs/Plant-trials-and-awards/Plant-bulletins/Hydrangea-paniculata

Orozco-Abando, W., G. N. Hirsch and H. Y. Wetzstein, 2005. Genotypic variation in Flower Induction and Development in *Hydrangea macrophylla*. Hort Science 40(6)1695-1698.

Porter, W. C. Hydrangeas for Mississippi gardens. 2015. Extension Service of Mississippi State University, Publication 2574. https://extension.msstate.edu/sites/default/files/publications/publications/p2574_1.pdf

Rosen, C. J. and D.B. White. 1999. "Preventing Pollution Problems from Lawn and Garden Fertilizers." University of Minnesota Extension Service. http://www.extension.umn.edu/distribution/horticulture/DG2923.html

Smith, S. Cercospora leaf spot of hydrangea. University of Arkansas Extension Publication FSA 7570. Revised 2017.

The United States National Arboretum, Hydrangea questions and answers. www.usna.usda.gov/Gardens/faqs/hydrangeafaq2.html

Wade, G. L. Growing Bigleaf Hydrangea. The University of Georgia College of Agricultural & Environmental Sciences, Cooperative Extension Service, Fact Sheet H-92-011, Athens, GA. http://extension.uga.edu/publications/detail.cfm?number=C973

Yeary, W. M. and A. Fulcher, 2013. A Tennessee Landscape Contractor's Guide to Hydrangeas. UT Extension University of Tennessee Publication # W304 12/13 14-0081. https://extension.tennessee.edu/publications/Documents/W304.pdf

Note: Links were current as of the publication of this book.

HYDRANGEA RESOURCES

ATTRACTING BENEFICIAL INSECTS TO YOUR GARDEN

Here is a link to an excellent IPM fact sheet on file from the University of California Cooperative Extension-Sacramento County about the wisdom of growing certain plants to attract beneficial insects: http://ucanr.edu/sites/sacmg/files/77452.pdf

If you need to bring in your beneficials, there are many mail-order suppliers available. Remember that timing is critical and that you need to have some bad bugs for them to eat so they don't fly away or worse, die.

Here are a few mail order companies; however, an internet search will yield many more.
ARBICO Organics
http://www.arbico-organics.com/

Beneficial Insectary, Inc.
http://www.insectary.com/

Peaceful Valley Farm & Garden Supply
https://www.groworganic.com/

Planet Natural
https://www.planetnatural.com/product-category/natural-pest-control/beneficial-insects/

Note: Links were current as of the publication of this book.

INFORMATIONAL SITES

https://www.LorraineBallato.com: Author website. Includes info about author, speaking topics and upcoming public speaking engagements, how to contact Lorraine , and the all important HYDRANGEA BLOG. This free blog contains valuable seasonal hydrangea information that is delivered to your inbox about twice a month just by subscribing. The site is also where you can order a signed copy of this book.

http://www.baileynurseries.com/gardeners/
Breeders and growers of widely recognized premier plants.

http://www.conweb.com/hydrangeas
Home of Pete's Hydrangeas.

http://www.endlesssummerblooms.com/
The home source of information about Endless Summer® hydrangeas, straight from the horse's mouth.

http://www.hydrangea.com

http://www.hydrangeashydrangeas.com/
Has good tips on drying hydrangeas and lots of other information.

http://www.provenwinners.com
Extraordinarily deep site about all things hydrangea.

https://www.aphis.usda.gov/aphis/home/
United States Animal and Plant Health Inspection Service (APHIS) a division of the United States Department of Agriculture. The agency that works to defend America's animal and plant resources from agricultural pests and diseases. Deep information source.

Note: Links were current as of the publication of this book.

HYDRANGEA ORGANIZATIONS

Alabama Hydrangea Society
http://www.alabamahydrangeasociety.org/
Meets at Aldridge Gardens in Hoover, Alabama

American Hydrangea Society
P. O. Box 53234
Atlanta, GA 30355
http://americanhydrangeasociety.org/

The Blue Ridge Hydrangea Society
P.O. Box 326
Horse Shoe, NC 28742
www.blueridgehydrangeasociety.org
For information, contact
Linda Shapiro, Society President & Founder
Email: blueflowers@blueridgehydraneasociety.org

The Cape Cod Hydrangea Society, Inc.
P. O. Box 681
South Dennis, MA 02660
Email: info@thecapecodhydrangeasociety.org

The Mid-South Hydrangea Society
635 West Dr.
Memphis, TN 38112
http://www.midsouthhydrangea.com/

St. Louis Hydrangea Society

542 Edgar Ct.

St. Louis, MO 63119

Phone: 314.954.7501

Email: reissk3@aol.com

http://www.stlouishydrangeasociety.org/

Note: Links were current as of the publication of this book

HYDRANGEA GARDENS TO VISIT

Aldridge Gardens http://aldridgegardens.com/
Hydrangea Garden, Dirr Collection
3530 Lorna Road
Hoover, AL 35216
Phone: 205.682.8019; E-Fax: 205.776.7833;
Email: info@aldridgegardens.com

Atlanta Botanical Garden http://atlantabg.org/explore/plant-
collections#section-hydrangea
1345 Piedmont Avenue
Atlanta, GA 30309
Phone: 404.876.5859

Brooklyn Botanic Garden www.bbg.org/
1000 Washington Avenue
Brooklyn, NY 11225
Phone: 718.622.4433

Gibbs Gardens https://www.gibbsgardens.com/garden-photos/hydrangea-
gardens/
1987 Gibbs Drive
Ball Ground, GA 30107
Phone: 770.893.1881

Heritage Museums & Gardens http://www.heritagemuseumsandgardens.org/
Home of the Cape Cod Hydrangea Society Display Garden
67 Grove Street
Sandwich, MA 02563
Phone: 508.888.3300; Email: info@heritagemuseums.org

New York Botanical Garden http://www.nybg.org/home/
2900 Southern Blvd.
Bronx, NY 10458
Phone: 718.817.8700

Norfolk Botanical Garden http://norfolkbotanicalgarden.org/explore/
Home to over 300 hydrangeas representing 20 different species and over 200
cultivars of hydrangeas
6700 Azalea Garden Rd.
Norfolk, VA 23518
Phone: 757.441.5830

Scott Arboretum of Swarthmore College http://www.scottarboretum.org/
gardens/featured.html
Home to more than 100 taxa, representing 15 species of hydrangeas
500 College Avenue
Swarthmore, PA 19081
Phone: 610.328.8025; Fax: 610.328.7755;
Email: scott@swarthmore.edu

Shamrock Collection www.hortensias-hydrangea.com/
Site of the French National collection and the largest collection of hydrangeas
in the world
Created by Corinne & Robert Mallet in France
Jardin Shamrock Collection nationale d'hydrangéas
Route du Manoir d'Ango
76119 Varengeville sur Mer
Varengeville-sur-Mer is near Dieppe on the coast of Upper Normandy
Phone: 011 (33) 2 35 85 14 64. Fax : 011 02 35 85 30 20
Email: shamrock76@wanadoo.fr

Smith-Gilbert Gardens http://smithgilbertgardens.com/
2382 Pine Mountain Road
Kennesaw, GA 30152
Phone: 770.919.0248

UGA Hydrangea Shade Garden www.uga.edu
University of Georgia, Department of Horticulture
Athens, GA 30602
Phone: 706.542.2471

United States National Arboretum www.usna.usda.gov
3501 New York Avenue NE
Washington, D.C. 20002
Phone: 202.245.2726

Van Dusen Botanical Garden http://vandusengarden.org/
5251 Oak Street
Vancouver, BC V6M 4H1
Canada
Phone: 604.878.9274

Woodlands Garden http://www.woodlandsgarden.org/
932 Scott Blvd.
Decatur, GA 30030
Phone: 404.373.2222

Note: Links were current as of the publication of this book

BRITISH GARDENS TO VISIT

I had the good fortune to live in England for a short time and whenever possible, garden visits were a prime pastime. The benign British climate produces magnificent *Hydrangea macrophyllas* regardless of where in the country they are grown. If you visit, do try to get to a few of these superb gardens when they are flowering and ask in the area you are visiting about others; they are everywhere.

Sir Harold Hillier Gardens http://www3.hants.gov.uk/hilliergardens/hillier-info.htm
Jermyns Lane
Romsey, Hampshire SO51 0QA
Phone: 011-44-01794 369317/318

Hydrangea Derby http://hydrangeaderby.co.uk
National Collection of Hydrangeas, the largest in the UK and the third largest in the world
Darley Abbey Park
Derby, UK
Phone: 011-44-01332 255828

Royal Botanic Gardens, Kew http://www.kew.org/
Richmond, Surrey TW9 3AE
Phone: 011-44-(0)20 8332 5000
Email: info@kew.org

Kiftsgate Court Gardens http://www.kiftsgate.co.uk/
Chipping Campden
Gloucestershire GL55 6LN
Phone: 011-44-01386 438 777
Email: info@kiftsgate.co.uk

RHS Garden, Wisley
Woking, Surrey
England, GU23 6QB
Phone: 011-44-01483 211113;
Email: wisleyplantcentre@rhs.org.uk

Trelissick Gardens
Feock (near Truro)
Cornwall TR3 6QL
Phone: 011-44-01872 862090;
Email: trelissick@nationaltrust.org.uk

Note: Links were current as of the publication of this book

MAIL-ORDER SUPPLIERS OF PLANTS

Digging Dog Nursery
P.O. Box 471
Albion, Canada 95410
Phone: 707.937.1130
https://diggingdog.com/

Forestfarm
990 Tetherow Road
Williams, OR 97544-9599
Phone: 541.846.7269
http://www.forestfarm.com/

Hydrangeas Plus®
P.O. Box 389
6543 S. Zimmerman Rd
Aurora, OR 97002
Phone: 866.433.7896
http://hydrangeasplus.com/

Rare Find Nursery
Purveyors of Fine Plants
957 Patterson Rd.
Jackson, NJ 08527
Phone: 732.833.0613
http://www.rarefindnursery.com/

Wilkerson Mill Gardens
Specializing in Hydrangeas
9595 Wilkerson Mill Rd.
Palmetto, GA 30268
Phone: 770.463.2400
http://www.hydrangea.com

Note: Links were current as of the publication of this book

BIBLIOGRAPHY

Boebel, Tim. Hydrangeas in the North: Getting Blooms in the Colder Climates. CreateSpace, 2011.

Church, Glyn and Pat Greenfield (Photographer). Hydrangeas. Firefly Books, Richmond Hill, ON 2001.

Church, Glyn. Complete Hydrangeas. Firefly Books, Richmond Hill, ON 2007.

Dirr, Michael A. and Bonnie L. Dirr (Illustrator). Hydrangeas for American Gardens. Timber Press, Portland, OR 2004.

Harrison, Joan. Hydrangeas: Cape Cod and the Islands. Schiffer Publishing, Ltd., Atglen, PA 2012.

Harrison, Joan. Heavenly Hydrangeas: A Practical Guide for the Home Gardener. Schiffer Publishing, Ltd., Atglen, PA 2013.

Haworth-Booth, Michael. The Hydrangeas. Constable and Company, Ltd. London, 1984.

Lawson-Hall Toni and Brian Rothera. Hydrangeas, A Gardener's Guide. Timber Press, Portland, OR 2005.

Mallet, Corinne. Hydrangeas, Species and Cultivars , Vol. 2. Florilegium, November 1992.

van Gelderen, C. J. and D. M. van Gelderen. Encyclopedia of Hydrangeas. Timber Press, Portland, OR 2004.

INDEX

References to photographs are bold.

rooting in water, 118–119
semi-ripe, 117–118, 154
softwood, 117–118, 154
stem, 154
tip, 155
when to take cuttings, 117–118

D

deadheading, **15**, 151
   See also pruning
deer, 37, 111–112
diatomaceous earth, 104
diseases
   anthracnose, 93, 149
   bacterial diseases, 97–98
   botrytis, 92, 150
   Cercospora leaf spot, 91–92
   fungal diseases, 91–96
   milky spore disease, 109
   powdery mildew, 93–94
   root rot, 96–97, 153
   rust, 94, 153
   treating fungal diseases, 94–96
disinfectants, 95
division, 118
dolomitic lime, 8–9
drainage
   improving, 62, 131
   testing, 75–76
      See also root rot
drought tolerance, 31

E

elemental sulfur, 10
everblooming, 151
   See also reblooming hydrangeas
exfoliating bark, 36

F

fertile, defined, 151
fertilizers
   balanced, 60, 62
   compost, **62**, 67, 76, 150
   defined, 151
   and lack of blooms, 25
   organic rose food, **63**
   and phosphorous, 9, 10

selecting, 60–61
slow-release, 154
fertilizing hydrangeas
   applying correctly, 61–62
   containerized plants, 63–64
   general guidelines, 59
   Hydrangea arborescens, 66–67
   Hydrangea macrophylla and *H. serrata*, 63–65
   Hydrangea paniculata, 67
   Hydrangea petiolaris, 66
   Hydrangea quercifolia, 65–66
   selecting the right fertilizer, 60–61
   soil testing, 59–60
   timing application, 61
   what fertilizing won't do, 62–63
Fine Gardening, 53
florets, defined, 151
floriferous, defined, 151
florist's hydrangea. *See Hydrangea macrophylla*
flowers
   blue, 9–10
   changing color of, 7–10
   defined, 151
   pink, 8–9
four-lined plant bugs, 106
free flowering. See reblooming hydrangeas
fungal diseases, 91–94
   treating, 94–96
      See also diseases; root rot
fungicides, 95–96

G

genus, defined, 151
glycoside amygdalin, 125
gray mold. *See* botrytis
groundcover. *See Hydrangea petiolaris*
growing on, defined, 151
growing zones. *See* climate zones

H

hand-picking insects, 102, 108
hardiness, 127–128
   map, **129**
      See also climate zones
heat tolerance, 131

organic fertilizers. *See* fertilizers
organic gardening, 101–103
oyster shell scale, 105

P

panicle hydrangea. *See Hydrangea paniculata*
panicles, 152
   See also Hydrangea paniculata
Pee Gee hydrangea. *See Hydrangea paniculata*
pests
   insects, 103–109
   Integrated Pest Management (IPM), 101–103
   wildlife, 111–112
petals, defined, 152
petioles, defined, 153
pH
   and changing flower color, 7–10
   defined, 153
   Hydrangea arborescens, 66
   Hydrangea macrophylla, 64
   Hydrangea paniculata, 67
   Hydrangea petiolaris, 66
   Hydrangea quercifolia, 65
   Hydrangea serrata, 64
   and iron deficiency, 8–9, 64
   overview, 6–7
   sensitivity, 8, 23
   and transplanting, 76
      See also soil
phosphorous, 9, 10, 59
   See also fertilizers
Phytophthora root rot, 96
pine needles, 8
pink flowers, 8–9
planting. *See* transplanting hydrangeas
poisoning, 125
potassium, 59
   See also fertilizers
potassium bicarbonate, 95
powdery mildew, **93**–94
   See also diseases
PPAF, 117
propagation
   division, 118
   layering, 121–123
   legalities, 117

rooting cuttings in a container, 119–121
rooting cuttings in water, 118–119
rooting hormones, 119–120, 153
vegetative, 155
when to take cuttings, 117–118
protective plants, 5
pruners, **12**–13
pruning
   3 Ds, 11–12, 34, 41, 49
   apical dominance, 18–19
   checklist, 20
   deadheading, 15
   defined, 153
   guidelines, 12
   Hydrangea arborescens, 41–43
   Hydrangea macrophylla, 10–11, 20
   Hydrangea paniculata, 49–54
   Hydrangea petiolaris, 38
   Hydrangea quercifolia, 34
   Hydrangea serrata, 10–11, 20
   reasons to prune, 11–12
   for size, 15
   timing, 13–14, 25
   tip pruning, 18–**19**
   tools, 12–13
   winterkill, 16–17
pruning saws, 13
puddling in, 77–78
Pythium root rot, 96

Q

quercifolia. *See Hydrangea quercifolia*
quick connect set-ups, **70**

R

rabbits, 111–112
reblooming hydrangeas, 11, 27–29
   and apical dominance, 18–19
   pruning varieties that bloom on old and new wood, 19–20
   in warmer climates, 132
remontant, defined, 153
repeat blooming. *See* reblooming hydrangeas
repellents, 153
root competition, 5, 131
root rot, 96, 153

treating, 97

    See also diseases

rooting cuttings. *See* propagation

rooting hormones, 119–**120**, 153

Royal Horticultural Society (RHS),

    Award of Garden Merit, 51

rust, 94, 153

    See also diseases

Rutgers Gardens, 53–54

S

sanitation, 12, 95, 97

scale, 105

semi-ripe cuttings, 117–118, 154

sepals, defined, 153

serrata. *See Hydrangea serrata*

serrated, defined, 153

shade

    dappled, 5

    full, 131

    Hydrangea arborescens, 40, 140

    Hydrangea macrophylla, 5

    Hydrangea paniculata, 46–47

    Hydrangea petiolaris, 36, 66, 144

    Hydrangea quercifolia, 33, 142

shoots, defined, 154

sidedressing, 154

Silverleaf hydrangea, 133

slow-release fertilizer, defined, 154

smooth hydrangea. *See Hydrangea
    arborescens*

Snowy hydrangea, 133

soaker hoses, **69**, **70**, **85**

    defined, 154

    and mulch, 85

softwood cuttings, 117–118

    defined, 154

soil

    acidic, 149

    alkaline, 149

    See also pH

soil acidifiers, 9–**10**

soil amendments

    adding when transplanting, 78

    to change flower color, 7–10

    defined, 154

    dolomitic lime, 8–9

    See also pH

soil collar, 132

soil testing, 59–60

    kits, **6**

sooty mold, 104, 105

species, defined, 154

spider mites, 105–106

standards, **46**, 133, 146, 154

stem cuttings, 154

    See also cuttings

stem hardiness, 17, 21, 34, 128

sterile, defined, 154

sticky traps, 102, 104

stippling, 105

stoma/stomata, defined, 154

suckers, 39, 154

sulfur, 10, 64

sun exposure, 25, 131

T

Tanglefoot®, 104

Teller series, 4

terminal, defined, 155

tip cuttings, 155

    See also cuttings

tip pruning, 18–**19**

    See also pruning

topiary. *See* standards

toxicity, 125

transplanting hydrangeas

    caring for a transplant, 78–79

    digging up and moving the plant,
    77–78, 81

    Hydrangea arborescens, 81–82

    Hydrangea macrophylla and *H. serrata*
    varieties, 79–80

    Hydrangea paniculata, 82–83

    Hydrangea petiolaris, 80–81

    Hydrangea quercifolia, 80

    mulching, 78

    overview, 75

    preparing the plant, 76–77, 81

    preparing the site, 75–76, 79–80, 81

    puddling in, 77–78

timing, 79, 80–83

trap plants, 108

trellises, defined, 155

PHOTO CREDITS

Cover Collage: Top two and bottom left: Pixabay. Across from title: Cityline®
Mars courtesy of Spring Meadow Nursery. Bottom right Strawberry Sundae
courtesy of Bailey Nurseries

Opposite Table of Contents: courtesy of Bailey Nurseries.

Introduction: Pixabay, with the exception of the hydrangea and daylilies photo

Page 2: Pixabay

Page 7: Wikimedia commons

Page 10: Soil acidifier courtesy of Espoma

Page 15: Deadheading: A. Ballato

Page 32: 'Little Honey' courtesy of Leonard Fultz of Dancing Oaks Nursery
and Gardens

Page 33: Courtesy of Bailey Nurseries

Page 37: 'Firefly' courtesy of Spring Meadow Nursery

Page 40: Hydrangea arborescens courtesy of Mt. Cuba Center

Page 43: Incrediball® courtesy of Proven Winners

Page 44: Photo courtesy of Bailey Nurseries

Page 47: Photo courtesy of Bailey Nurseries

Page 48: Pinky Winky® courtesy of Proven Winners; Angels Blush® courtesy
of Proven Winners

Page 49: Photo courtesy of Ball Horticultural

Page 58: Photo courtesy of Proven Winners

Page 62: Photo courtesy of Coast of Maine

Pages 63 & 64: Photos courtesy of Espoma

Page 74: Photo courtesy of Proven Winners

Page 84: Photo courtesy of Proven Winners

Page 88: Photo courtesy of Bailey Nurseries

Page 91: Photo courtesy of Fulya Baysal-Gurel

Page 93: Anthracnose, courtesy of Dr. Mark Whitman, University of
Tennessee; Powdery mildew, courtesy of Fulya Baysal-Gurel

Page 98: Photo courtesy of the Missouri Botanical Garden

Page 107: Japanese Beetle Life Cycle courtesy Joel Floyd, APHIS, PPQ

Page 110: Photo courtesy of Proven Winners

Page 114: Photo courtesy of Proven Winners

Page 116: Photo courtesy of Bailey Nurseries

Page 129: USDA Plant Hardiness Zone Map, 2012. Agricultural

Research Service, U.S. Department of Agriculture. Accessed from http://planthardiness.ars.usda.gov.

Page 130: Photo courtesy of Plants Nouveau

Page 133: Photo courtesy of Proven Winners

Page 135: Endless Summer® courtesy of Bailey Nurseries; Midnight Duchess® courtesy of Gardeners Confidence

Page 136: Let's Dance® Moonlight courtesy of Proven Winners

Page 137: Photo courtesy of Bailey Nurseries

Page 138: Tiny Tuff Stuff™ courtesy of Proven Winners

Page 140: Lime Rickey®, Invincibelle® Spirit, courtesy of Proven Winners

Page 141: 'Bounty' Photo courtesy of Bailey Nurseries

Page 142: Gatsby Gal® courtesy of Proven Winners; Jetstream™ courtesy of Bailey Nurseries

Page 145: Bobo® courtesy of Proven Winners; Baby Lace® courtesy of Gardeners Confidence

Page 146: Fire Light® courtesy of Proven Winners

Page 148: courtesy of Proven Winners

Author Photo: A. Ballato

Back Cover: Top left to right – Pixabay, Lorraine Ballato, Lorraine Ballato

Back Cover: Bottom photo courtesy of Bailey Nurseries

All other photos credit to the author.

One last look at some magnificent hydrangeas

MEET LORRAINE BALLATO

Lorraine's obsession with plants is evident through her lectures, social media writing, magazine articles, and photographs, which you can find in **Connecticut Gardener, Edible Nutmeg**, and elsewhere. She is an instructor at the New York Botanical Garden and for the Connecticut Master Gardener Program, as well as for the Federated Garden Clubs of Connecticut. Her weekly gardening columns ran for more than ten years, reaching more than 15,000 homes in northwest Connecticut. She even wrote copy for the section on "woodies" for a couple of the White Flower Farm Spring catalogs. Lorraine's previous book is *Successful Self Watering Containers: Converting Your Favorite Container to a Self-Waterer*, another of her favorite subjects.

As a professional horticulturist, Lorraine has been a guest on numerous gardening radio programs from Alaska to Connecticut. She speaks at regional symposia, flower shows, and to civic groups and garden clubs, creating talks that are both instructive and highly entertaining on a broad range of subjects tailored to each audience.

In her role as an Advanced Master Gardener, Lorraine works with a sizeable team of gardeners of all levels in a 3,000-square-foot organic fruit and vegetable garden in Fairfield County, Connecticut. From April through October each year, the garden grows and annually donates nearly 700 pounds of produce to homeless shelters and food banks. It also trains Master Gardener interns and assists the gardening public weekly.

Besides tending the Connecticut garden that Lorraine and her husband have created (including many plants under trial conditions), Lorraine's organic home garden includes seasonal vegetables, her beloved hydrangeas, and all manner of ornamentals, which have informed her writing, lectures, and radio guest spots. Their garden is not only a laboratory, but it has been the subject of magazine articles and has been featured on several garden tours.

CPSIA information can be obtained
at www.ICGtesting.com
Printed in the USA
BVHW061951080721
611480BV00002B/35